60344547

E5
1094

International Trade Law

GW00707270

International Trade Law

Janette Charlery
LLB (Hons), MA, Cert H Ed

THE M & E HANDBOOK SERIES

Pitman Publishing
128 Long Acre, London WC2E 9AN

A Division of Longman Group UK Limited

First published 1993

© Longman Group UK Limited 1993

British Library Cataloguing in Publication Data
A catalogue record for this book is available from the British Library

ISBN 0 7121 1192 1

All rights reserved; no part of this publication may be reproduced,
stored in a retrieval system, or transmitted in any form or by any
other means, electronic, mechanical, photocopying, recording, or
otherwise without either the prior written permission of the
Publishers or a licence permitting restricted copying in the United Kingdom
issued by The Copyright Licensing Agency Ltd, 90 Tottenham
Court Road, London W1P 9HE. This book may not be lent, resold, hired
out or otherwise disposed of by way of trade in any form of binding
or cover than that in which it is published, without the prior
consent of the Publishers.

Typeset by FDS Ltd, Penarth
Printed and bound in Singapore

This book is dedicated to my parents

Contents

Acknowledgements

Sincere gratitutde to Reenie, George and their children Hector, Stephen, Carol and Patricia for their encouragement and belief in my ability.

I would also like to express my thanks to Mrs Linda Howes who patiently converted my many handwritten drafts into manuscript form, to Mr Richard Royale for his help in locating much of the information needed and to the editorial staff at Pitman.

However, pride of place must go to my husband Delroy who has been my inspiration throughout, without whom this book would not have been possible.

Table of cases

Table of statutes

Table of conventions and rules

1
Cost Insurance Freight contracts

Introduction

1. Two features of Cost Insurance Freight contracts

The term 'Cost Insurance Freight' always relates to the destination of goods. For example, if a seller sends goods to a buyer 'Cost Insurance Freight Charleston', then the destination will be Charleston.

When a price is agreed on Cost Insurance Freight terms, then the price the buyer is charged covers:

(a) the cost of the goods;
(b) the insurance of the goods to their Cost Insurance Freight destination;
(c) the freight for carrying the goods to their Cost Insurance Freight destination.

2. The two main elements of Cost Insurance Freight contracts

The first point above relates to what is included in the price. The second and third relate to the nature of the seller's delivery obligations.

Dual Obligations

3. The seller's obligations under a Cost Insurance Freight contract

The seller's obligations under a Cost Insurance Freight contract are heavier than a buyer's. The seller has dual obligations to:

(a) *The goods.* The seller must either ship or buy goods already afloat that are contract conforming. Also, the seller must arrange for the insurance of the goods to their Cost Insurance Freight destination.
(b) *The documents.* The seller must tender certain documents to the buyer. The three main documents are:

    (i) *the invoice*;
    (ii) *the Bill of Lading;*
    (iii) *the insurance policy.*

Once the seller has performed the obligations in relation to the goods and the documents, along with any additional ones mentioned in the contract, he has fully performed and fulfilled his obligations under a Cost Insurance Freight contract and is then entitled to receive payment. This is regardless of what happens to the goods after shipment as the seller does not guarantee that the goods will reach their destination. The seller's risk ends on shipment, after which the risk is transferred to the buyer — *see Horst* v. *Biddell Bros* (1912) (1:5).

4.   The two intents of a Cost Insurance Freight contract

The primary intent is for the seller to transfer to the buyer the goods referred to in the contract of sale.

The secondary intent is to cover the seller if the goods are lost or destroyed along the way. Because the seller has transferred his rights to the buyer through the Bill of Lading, the buyer can sue the carrier and has rights under an insurance policy for the goods.

5.   The nature of Cost Insurance Freight contracts

Once the seller has performed his obligations, then the buyer must pay the seller against the documents once they are tendered. In due course, when the goods arrive, the buyer must accept them. This is the case *even if* the goods are lost or destroyed by the time the documents are tendered. The buyer must still accept the correct documents tendered and pay against them, even though he or she knows that the goods are lost.

The case of *Horst* v. *Biddell Bros* (1912) clarifies the nature of a Cost Insurance Freight contract. It was held that the seller had fulfilled his obligations when he tendered the documents to the buyer and so payment had to be made.

The seller has dual obligations —

Hindley v. *East Indian Produce Co. Ltd* (1973): There was a cost and freight contract (see 1:**15**) for 50 tonnes of jute cost and freight Breham with a shipment period of October to December.

    In the following January, standard shipping documents were sent to the buyer and included a Bill of Lading dated 31 December, which said jute had been shipped on board from Bangkok. The buyer paid against the document. However, when the vessel arrived there were no goods. The buyer sued the seller for the price he had paid due to non-shipment.

The seller put forward three arguments:

(a) he was not liable because it was a cost and freight contract, which is only a sale of documents rather than a contract for the sale of goods, so the Bill of Lading was proper on the face of it;

(b) he was not liable as they were parties in a string who had bought the goods afloat and so he was not the original shipper;

(c) the buyer must be limited to such remedies as he may have against the carrier.

It was held by Kerr J. in response to the seller's arguments that:

(a) it is an implied term of any such contract that the Bill of Lading should appear proper on its face and that the statements made within be true and accurate;

(b) the seller or shipper were in breach of the obligation either to ship or to procure the shipment of contract goods as none had been shipped;

(c) it was immaterial that there may be a remedy against the carrier.

Thus, the buyer was entitled to his money back because the seller had not performed his duality of obligations, i.e. his obligation to tender the documents *and* to ship the goods. In this case the documents were tendered but no goods were shipped. In addition, the documents were incorrect as there was no true Bill of Lading.

Consider the following. Why did the buyer sue the seller instead of the carrier? There are a few possible answers to this question. For example, the jurisdiction or the fact that the carrier could be judgment proof or that the assets may be in the jurisdiction of the seller.

Really it is due to the rule in *Grant* v. *Norway* (1851) that the shipmaster does not have the authority to sign for non-existent goods. The Hague Visby Rules do not affect this *Grant* v. *Norway* rule or s. 1 of the Bills of Lading Act 1855.

6. Judicial definitions of a Cost Insurance Freight contract

There have been many judicial definitions of a Cost Insurance Freight contract, but the one most often quoted was put forward by Bankson L.J. in the *Arnold Karberge* case.

Arnold Karberge v. *Blythe, Green, Jourdain* (1916). There were two contracts providing for the sale of beans Cost Insurance

Freight Naples to Rotterdam. Contract A, had a
German-issued bill of lading and a UK insurance policy and
both were tendered. In contract B, both the bill of lading and
insurance policy were of German origin.

A war broke out, but the seller still tendered the documents.
The buyer refused to accept the documents and pay the price.

It was held that by reason of the Trading with the Enemy
Act (1939), the tendering of documents was void. The seller
must tender valid and effective documents that will enable the
buyer to deal with the carrier and, as these were not so
tendered, the buyer was justified in refusing to accept the
documents.

Scrutton J. at first instance said the 'Cost Insurance Freight contract
is not a sale of goods but the sale of documents relating to these goods'
whereas Bankson L.J., on appeal, stated that the Cost Insurance
Freight contract is a contract for the sale of goods to be performed
by the delivery of the documents.

Professor Schmitthoff looked at the contract from an economic
point of view and concluded that the Cost Insurance Freight contract
is for the sale of documents rather than goods because of the use of
string contracts. From a legal point of view, however, this is not the
case, as illustrated by the *Arnold Karberge* and the *Hindley* cases *(ante)*,
i.e. it relates to the sale of goods to be performed by the delivery of
documents.

This is reinforced by the Sale of Goods Act 1979. If Cost Insurance
Freight contracts did not apply to the sale of goods, then the Sale of
Goods Act would not apply either.

In *Comptoir d'Achat* v. *Luis de Ridder (The Julia)* (1949), Lord Porter
set out the essential features of a Cost Insurance Freight contract
(although the case concerned Arrival contracts). These are that the
seller is responsible for the:

(a) shipment of the goods;
(b) arranging the carriage document;
(c) arranging the insurance document;
(d) arranging the tender of documents.

These obligations of the seller are discussed next and in the chapters
that follow.

Shipment

7. Sale of Goods Act 1979

According to s. 13(i) of the Act, where there is a contract for the sale of goods by description, there is an implied condition that the goods will correspond to the description. This section has given rise to much litigation.

What constitutes an element of description of the goods under s. 13 of the Sale of Goods Act? The elements are usually:

(a) duality;
(b) form of packaging;
(c) time of shipment of the goods.

Goods must comply with their description —

> *Manbre Saccharine Co.* v. *Corn Products Co.* (1919): The case concerned a Cost Insurance Freight contract for starch to be shipped in 280 lb bags. The correct total quantity was shipped but in the wrong bag weights. The buyer noticed the difference on the Bill of Lading and rejected the documents. It was held that the buyer was entitled to reject the documents as the goods, having been packed in the wrong bags, did not correspond with their description in the contract of sale. The size of the bags formed part of the description of the goods and there was no correspondence. Failure to correspond with description is therefore a major breach of the contract.
> It was also said *obiter* that if these valid grounds for rejection of the goods had not existed, i.e. if the seller had tendered the proper documents, the seller could still demand payment even though at the time of tender the ship had sunk and the seller knew that it had.
>
> *Tradax* v. *European Grain* (1983): This concerns the description in a contract of sale of soya beans. A clause said 'for USA toasted soya bean meal — maximum 7.5 per cent fibre', but the cargo on arrival had excess of 7.5 per cent. It was held that 7.5 per cent formed part of the description of the goods so the buyer could reject them.

There has also been litigation based on s. 14 of the Sale of Goods Act 1979 in Cost Insurance Freight and cost and freight contracts, i.e. regarding the term that the goods under the contract must be of merchantible quality, that they must be reasonably fit for the purpose for which they are required —

> *Mash & Murrell* v. *Joseph Emanuel Ltd* (1961): This concerned a cost and freight contract for potatoes to be shipped from Cyprus to England. The seller had bought them afloat. On

arrival at their destination, they were rotten and unfit for human consumption. The seller was sued by the buyer.

The issue was what had caused the rot. Was it caused by the failure of the carrier to ventilate the goods properly or did it occur as a result of damp, etc. on the ship?

It was held that the potatoes were shipped in good condition but were not properly ventilated. The seller was liable to the buyer for breach of the terms implied in the contract under s. 14 of the Sale of Goods Act 1979 that the goods are to be reasonably fit for the purpose for which they are required.

Lord Diplock's judgment in this case therefore means that when goods are sold under a Cost Insurance Freight contract that involves shipment, there is an implied term that the goods be of merchantable quality when put on board and that they must remain merchantable for a reasonable amount of time after transit and delivery.

Terms

8. Classification of terms

Usually terms are either a *warranty* or binding, a *condition*, but not all terms can be classified this way. Some terms can only be classified after waiting to see how serious the breach has been — these are called *innominate terms*. Only with the 'wait and see' approach can it be determined whether the term has been a warranty or a condition —

Cehave v. *Bremer Handelgesellschaft (The Hansa Nord)* (1975):
The contract was for 1200 tons of citrus pulp pellets Cost Insurance Freight Rotterdam. A clause in the contract was, 'Shipment to be made in good condition'. The buyer paid upon tender of the shipping documents but, when the vessel arrived in Rotterdam, only part of the goods were aboard and some of these were damaged.
The buyer rejected the whole shipment and demanded that the seller refund the money he had been paid. The seller refused.
Following the buyer's rejection of the goods, they were bought and re-sold in a chain but ended up back in the original buyer's possession. He had arranged for these intermediaries to purchase the goods to save money.
It was held that the term was an innominate term. The goods

could still be used for their original intent of feeding the buyer's pigs and so the breach did not go to the root of the contract. Therefore it was a warranty and repudiation of the contract by the buyer was unjustified because the goods were still of merchantible quality in accordance with s. 14 of the Sale of Goods Act 1979.

NOTE: A buyer may still reject goods *even though* he has accepted the relevant documents if the goods do not correspond with the contract.

An issue to consider is whether a seller can ship all the goods on the same vessel in bulk or whether there can be partial shipments of the total order —

Cobec Brazilian Trading v. *Toepfer* (1983): There was a contract for the sale of soya beans: 19000 tonnes to Santango in Spain and 5000 to Seville, Spain.
10 July was the last possible date for the shipment, but the 19000 tonne load was loaded by then, not the 5000, which was not loaded until 14 July.
The seller tendered the Bills of Lading to the buyer but the buyer rejected the lot. The question was, did the buyer have to accept the Seville Bill of Lading or could they be treated separately?
It was held that the buyer could not sever the Bill of Lading as it was for *one* contract on the *same* ship, although for different destinations. If he wanted to reject it, he would have to reject everything, as the whole quantity was not shipped in time, i.e. by 10 July.

Procuring goods afloat

9. Buying afloat
The seller can either arrange shipment of the goods with an agent or supplier if he cannot ship them personally, as long as he arranges the shipment, or the seller can buy a cargo on its way to the Cost Insurance Freight destination, i.e. he may buy the goods *afloat*. However, these goods must fit the description in the documents and be shipped on the correct date, otherwise the buyer can reject the goods or documents. The goods must be contract conforming —

Fairclough Dodd & Jones v. *Vandol* (1955): McNair J. stressed that *force majeure* clauses do not discharge the seller from his obligations. He cannot plead an export ban as a reason for his non-performance of the contract because, although *shipping* the goods was barred, he may be able to perform by buying goods already shipped, i.e. goods afloat.

The seller's obligations will only be discharged if he can show that:

(a) he could not ship the goods; and
(b) he could not buy goods afloat because they were outside the contract period —

> *Lewis Emmanuel* v. *Summutt* (1959): this concerned a contract for potatoes to be shipped Cost Insurance Freight London on or by 24 April. When the seller came to arrange the carriage, there was only one vessel calling at London via Malta and it was fully booked.
> It was held by Pearson J. that the seller should have foreseen this occurrence and bought afloat. It was not a frustrating event. He should have arranged for shipment himself or by an agent or afloat within the contract shipping period.

Place and time of shipment

10. Place of shipment

Place of shipment clauses within a contract are usually condition-type terms. Cost Insurance Freight will always be a destination term, but sometimes contracts will also give the *origin* of the goods.

Why is there a need for an origin term? From the buyer's point of view:

(a) there may be a national prohibition on goods originating from certain countries; or
(b) there may be regional integration arrangements, e.g., if goods are available in the EC then they should be shipped from there to avoid tariffs on the goods.

From the seller's point of view:

(a) the doctrine of frustration (*see* Chapter 11) will relieve the seller from any further liability.

11. Time of shipment

Time of shipment is also a conditional term when it appears in a contract. This is regarded as part of the description of the goods. Failure to ship on time gives the buyer the right to reject the documents and the goods.

Usually shipment takes place too late and the contract is repudiated but the same will apply if shipment is too early —

> *Bowes v. Shand* (1877): This case concerned a Cost Insurance Freight contract for rice to be shipped from Madras in March or April. The seller shipped at the end of February.
> It was held that the buyer could reject the goods as they were not shipped within the specified time so there was a major breach. The contract could be rescinded although, really, the buyer had rejected due to a fall in the price.

There are sound policy reasons for this principle:

(a) many Cost Insurance Freight contracts say cash against documents, but if the shipment is too early, then the documents will be ready earlier than the buyer expects and he may not yet have the cash to pay against the documents;
(b) if, for example, rice or flour is shipped too early to the buyer, then he will have to pay additional costs for warehouse storage space, which is unnecessary.

If a Bill of Lading is incorrectly dated, but the buyer accepts the documents and then realises the false date, he may still reject the goods on their arrival.

Whether the buyer rejects the goods or not will usually depend on the market price as it may be better to accept them than to reject them fully.

If the time of shipment is not specified then it must be within a reasonable time of the making of the contract — *see Landauer* v. *Craven & Speeding Bros* (1912).

The route

12. Contractually agreed routes

If there has been a contractually agreed route to carry the goods, then it will become a condition-type term of the contract and must be followed — *Re an arbitration between Sutro & Heilbut Symons & Co.*

If there has not been a contractually agreed route, then there will be an implied term that the goods will be carried along the usual or customary route from the port of shipment to the Cost Insurance Freight destination.

This ordinary or usual or customary route is not to be determined at the time of contracting but when the seller comes to perform his obligation.

13. Non-contractually agreed routes

Tsakiroglou v. *Noble Thorl* (1962): The contract was for the sale of goods to be shipped from the Sudan to Hamburg. When the contract was made, the usual route was through the Suez Canal but, before the time of performance, it was closed. The usual route, therefore, became unavailable and the seller failed to ship the goods. The seller contended that he was justified in doing so by reason of the doctrine of frustration and the dramatic increase in the cost of performing the contract.

It was held that the time for determination is not the time of *contracting* but the time of the seller's *performance*. The seller was therefore in breach. The route not being available was not a defence as the seller could have taken another route, although it would have taken longer and been more expensive. The contract was not frustrated as a result of the closure of the Suez route, so the seller was in breach of the condition and contract.

It was in this case that Lord Radcliffe used his famous door analogy:

If a man is used to leaving through his front door for his appointments, then he has no excuse why he should not use the back door if the front door does not work.

In the above case there was nothing in the contract specifying the date on which the goods were to arrive so a longer route was acceptable, but what if an arrival date had been specified? Then the longer route would not have been a possibility, so specifying a date can restrict the choice of routes that can be used.

14. Calling at other ports

Another issue is whether a vessel can call at other ports along the way to its Cost Insurance Freight destination or whether it should go direct —

Bergerco v. *Vergoil* (1984): The final contract said that the goods were to be shipped direct to Bombay. The ship called elsewhere, arriving late. The buyer accepted the Bill of Lading but afterwards realised that the shipment was not direct and the buyer sued the seller.

It was held that the terms of the contract said that the shipment was to be direct.

It will therefore depend on the terms of the contract as to whether the vessel is to go direct or may call at other ports on the way.

The seller has to tender certain carriage documents as part of his Cost Insurance Freight obligations. The main ones are:

(a) the Bill of Lading;
(b) the insurance policy; and
(c) the invoice.

Variants of Cost Insurance Freight contracts

15. Contracts in practice

Sometimes a contract is described as being a Cost Insurance Freight contract whereas in real terms it is something quite different —

Comptoir d'Achat v. *Luis de Ridder (The Julia)* (1949): The House of Lords held that although the sellers sold the goods on Cost Insurance Freight terms, the contract, in law, was an *Arrival contract*. This was mainly because the payment was not made for the documents but as an advance payment for a contract to be performed afterwards.

Other examples of where a contract would not be truly Cost Insurance Freight arise when the tender of the *goods* is admitted as an alternative to the tender of *documents* or if a transport document, for example, a Bill of Lading, does not transfer direct rights against a carrier to claim the goods.

Under a *cost and freight contract* it is the seller who has the obligation to arrange for the goods to be sent to a port of shipment that will be named in each individual contract.

The seller also has the obligation to meet all costs and freight charges for such transactions. This appears to be similar to the traditional Cost Insurance Freight contract, but with a cost and freight contract, the seller is under no obligation to arrange the insurance for the goods ordered.

If the seller arranges insurance on behalf of the buyer, then this must be paid for separately, otherwise the only obligation that a seller has in this regard is to notify the buyer that the goods are in transit. This will then enable the buyer to arrange his own insurance, the goods then travelling at the buyer's risk.

It is common to find a clause in such contracts stipulating 'insurance is to be effected by the buyer'. If this is present, then it becomes an obligation of the seller, as in the case of *Golodetz* v. *Czarnikow Rionda (The Galatia)* (1981).

Under *Cost Insurance Freight and commission contracts* an intermediary acts on behalf of the overseas buyer. The price the customer has to pay also includes a commission for acting in such a capacity, as well as the usual cost, insurance and freight charges incurred.

Under *Cost Insurance Freight and exchange contracts* as well as paying for the cost, insurance and freight charges for goods, the customer also has to pay a charge to the bank based on current exchange rates.

Progress test 1

1. What are the obligations, under Common Law, of a seller and a buyer under a Cost Insurance Freight (CIF) contract? **(3, 5)**

2. Is a CIF contract based on delivery of the goods or the documents? **(4)**

3. What are the main documents that a buyer needs to accept goods delivered? **(3)**

4. What is the rule in *Grant* v. *Norway* (1851)? **(5)**

5. What are the elements of description under the Sale of Goods Act 1979? **(7)**

6. What is a place of shipment clause and why may they be important to a buyer? **(10)**

7. Under what circumstances may a contractually agreed route be departed from? **(12, 13)**

2
Arrival contracts

1. The nature of an Arrival contract

The essence of an Arrival contract, as one would expect from the name, is that it always pertains to the goods *arriving*. As with a Cost Insurance Freight contract, there is a contractual destination, but beyond that there is very little similarity.

2. The main differences

The main differences are that under a Cost Insurance Freight-type contract, the risk passes on shipment and the seller has the obligation to insure the goods whereas under an Arrival contract the risk only passes on the physical delivery of the goods at the destination contracted and there is no obligation on the seller to insure the goods as they travel at his risk to the destination —

Yangtsze Insurance Association v. *Tukmanjee* (1918): The contract was for teak logs. There was a trade and payment term in the contract stating 'ex ship payment against documents'. The subject matter of the contract was 144 teak logs, which were part of a larger shipment of 382 logs that had been shipped from Bangkok to Columbia.
The seller had insured all the 382 logs with Yangtsze Insurance Association, the insurance covering 'craft and raft risks' until the goods reached shore.
The buyer paid for the logs and took delivery ex ship, but, while the goods were afloat in the form of rafts tied together, they were driven out to sea. The buyer considered the logs as lost and sued under the insurance policy.
It was held by the Privy Council that the insurance policy could not be effected on behalf of the buyer or to cover his interest and so he had no right of claim under the insurance policy against the seller. The buyer could not take over the

seller's policy as he should have covered the risk from when delivery took place, ex ship.

Lord Summer pointed out that mere documents do not take the place of the goods, as documents are not the subject matter of the contract. The policy had been intended to cover the seller's interests only.

Here 'craft and raft' risks were covered as it was the practice of the seller to do this — it gave him maximum flexibility, allowing him to enter into safe contracts in which the term 'trade' could have been interpreted as 'landed' rather than 'ex ship'.

3.   Uncertainties

However, there have been cases where it is unclear as to the nature of the buyer's and seller's obligations regardless of the designation put on the contract — *see Comptoir d'Achat* v. *Luis de Ridder* (1949) (The Julia). The contract in this case, although *described* as Cost Insurance Freight, was really an Arrival contract. There was a contract for 500 tons of rye Cost Insurance Freight Antwerp, but the contract also included some unusual characteristics:

(a) the obligation fell on the seller to make a price adjustment for any deficiency in the landed weight;

(b) there was an expressed guarantee relating to the condition of the rye on arrival in Antwerp;

(c) the delivery order was issued by one seller's agent to another seller's agent in Antwerp to deliver goods when they arrived and there was a documentary substitution clause allowing delivery order and insurance certificates to be used instead of a Bill of Lading and insurance policy;

(d) the buyer and seller had been contracting on the same terms for a number of years and, in previous performances of the contract, the seller had tendered delivery orders that were not ships delivery orders but had been regularly accepted by the buyer.

While the ship was at sea on its way to Antwerp, Germany invaded Belgium and occupied the Antwerp port. The ship was therefore diverted to Lisbon where the cargo was discharged and sold by the seller. The seller informed the buyer of this and said that he was holding the proceeds of the sale for the buyer's account. This amount was lower than what the buyer had paid against tender of the documents. The buyer therefore sued for return of the original price.

If the contract had been Cost Insurance Freight, then the buyer would not have been entitled to do this as the seller would have performed his obligations by tendering the correct documents. If the contract had been an Arrival contract, then, according to its terms, the seller would have failed to ensure the goods' arrival and so the buyer would have been entitled to the original price paid.

In the *Comptoir d'Achat* case it was held that there was a price term that said what was to be included in the price of the goods. By looking at the parties' past practice and intentions, it was considered to be, in fact, an Arrival contract. Therefore, the buyer had the right to return of the original price.

A Cost Insurance Freight designation may have an unusual context —

> *Holland Columbo Trading Society* v. *Alawdeen* (1954): The contract was for the sale of goods stated to have a Cost Insurance Freight destination of Columbo on a cash against documents basis. Clause 1 of the contract stated 'any tender or delivery of the goods or Bill of Lading or delivery order or document as will enable us to obtain possession of the goods will be a valid tender of delivery'. There were other clauses in the contract, the effect of which was that the contract could be performed either through the tender of documents — Clause 1 — or through physical delivery — Clause 4 — of the goods.
>
> There was an invalid tendering of documents, so they were rejected by the buyer, but there was also a valid delivery of the goods, which the buyer had also rejected as not being contract conforming.
>
> It was held that this was a hybrid contract that could be performed or satisfied through the delivery of goods or through the tender of documents.

It will, therefore, not be a true Cost Insurance Freight contract if tender of the goods is different to the tender of documents and if the seller's liability is said to end on trans-shipment. Should the seller guarantee that goods will arrive, then he still has the risk. If the goods are to be delivered to a Cost Insurance Freight destination, the same rule applies. For example, Cost Insurance Freight contracts may provide that, on arrival, the goods are to be weighed or tested and the price will be fixed by reference to this delivered weight. It is quite common to have such a clause in a Cost Insurance Freight contract, along with maybe a price adjustment clause.

Progress test 2

1. What are the main differences between an Arrival contract and a contract based on cost, insurance and freight?   **(1, 2)**

2. Give an example of a case based on an Arrival contract. **(2, 3)**

3

The documents

Introduction

1. What makes documents of good tender?

For the documents to be of good tender under a Cost Insurance Freight contract, they must be valid and effective, enabling the buyer to have legally enforceable rights against the carrier and have control of the goods — *see Arnold Karberge* v. *Blythe, Green, Jourdain* (1916).

Specific elements

2. Correction clauses

The buyer must scrutinise the documents because once he accepts them, he has, in effect, also accepted any discrepancy in them and he cannot, therefore, later reject the goods. The conditions of a Cost Insurance Freight sale cannot be waived by a correction clause —

Siat v. *Tradax* (1980): A clause in the contract said:

If any document whatsoever required to be furnished by the seller is missing or in apparent contradiction with the clauses and condition of the sale contract and/or if such documents contain errors or omissions of any kind, the buyer must nevertheless perform and take up the documents if the seller gives written or cable notice to the buyer that the seller guarantees performance in accordance with the clauses and conditions of the contract.

The seller had tendered the documents but the Bill of Lading was defective as it had the wrong destination written on it.

It was held that the Bill of Lading was incorrect and so the buyer could reject it. The seller had assured the buyer that things were fine through a letter of guarantee and the seller had relied on this, contending that the buyer could not reject. The clause did not guarantee performance in accordance with the clauses and terms of the contract, it only guaranteed to cover the buyer for losses that may occur in costs and expenses. Therefore, the courts will not give effect to such correction clauses.

Gill & Duffus v. *Berger* (1984): The contract contained a conclusive evidence clause, saying, 'A certificate of quality issued by the inspector at the port of discharge shall be final'. The seller tendered the shipping documents to the buyer who rejected them as no certificate of quality had been issued, although the goods had not yet arrived.
It was held that this was an unjustified rejection as the certificate is not required until the goods have arrived at their destination, also a certificate of quality is not one of the shipping documents required to form part of the seller's documents to receive payment.

3. Goods already lost

A seller can tender documents if they are proper under a Cost Insurance Freight contract *even though*, before tender, the ship may have sunk to the bottom of the sea, and the seller knew at the time of tender that the goods were already lost. This is regularly accepted as good law.

McArthy J. in *Manbre Saccharine Co.* v. *Corn Products Co.* (1919) stated that, 'The contingency of loss is within and not outside the contemplation of the parties to a Cost Insurance Freight contract'.

Under a Cost Insurance Freight contract, risk in the goods passes, on shipment, to the buyer, so the goods travel at the buyer's risk once correct documents have been tendered. If the correct documents are not tendered, then the risk will remain with the seller — *see Groam* v. *Barber* (1915).

4. Time of tender

Early authority on this states that the shipping documents are to be tendered within a reasonable time after receipt.

The main case for this principle is *Saunders* v. *McLean* (1883) in which Lord Brett said that this reasonable time rule means reasonable exertion after the vessel is asail. If the goods are perishable, then the effort must be greater so that the documents are available *before* the ship arrives, enabling the discharging of the goods from the ship to take place as quickly as possible.

Horst v. *Biddell Bros* (1912) lays down the principle that tender and payment are to be done before the arrival of the goods. However, sometimes there may be a contractual provision as to the time of tender. These provisions are usually condition-type terms, especially in commercial contracts as time is considered to be of the essence.

> *Toepfer* v. *Verheijodens Veervveder Commissiehandel* (1980): The contract was Cost Insurance Freight Rotterdam for the sale of rape seed. The contract included a payment clause:
>
> Payment: net cash against documents and/or delivery order on arrival of the vessel at port of discharge but not later than 20 days after day of Bill of Lading. . .
>
> On 11 December 1974, a Bill of Lading was issued on shipment, but the carrying ship was grounded and suffered serious damage. On 20 December 1974, the goods were trans-shipped.
> In April 1975, the goods arrived in Europe and on 7 February 1975 the sub-buyer received the shipping documents but rejected them as they were presented out of time.
> The courts also held that the documents were tendered out of time. Despite the grounding, it had no effect on the seller's obligation to tender. The clause was breached and, because the provisions in the clause amounted to a condition-type term, the breach meant that the buyer could rescind the contract.
> The view of Donaldson L.J. was that the obligations imposed by the 'payment against document' clause were mutual and defined not in the latest or earliest date for payment but in the actual date. The clause was binding on both parties and was a condition of the contract.

On the other hand, the buyer may waive strict compliance with the condition if presentation of the documents is made *close* to the time, in which case, he cannot later treat the untimely production as a breach of the condition —

> *The Euromental* (1981): The contract contained a clause stipulating, 'Payment in cash . . . in exchange for shipping documents . . . If shipping documents have not been sighted at time of vessel's arrival, . . . sellers shall provide other

documents . . . entitling buyers to claim delivery of the
goods . . . and payment must be in exchange for same'.
The facts of the case were that the seller sold the buyer a
quantity of Spanish barley Cost Insurance Freight one safe
port, west coast of Italy. The contract was concluded on
GAFTA form 61, which provides for cash against the shipping
documents.

On 28 May, the barley was shipped and on 30 May the ship
arrived in Italy, but the shipping documents were not
available. The buyer refused to take delivery as the barley was
infested with live weevils. The buyer did not refuse it outright
but insisted that the seller fumigate the barley at his expense
— $10 000.

On 23 June, the seller tendered the documents, but the buyer
rejected them so the seller sold at a loss and sought to recover
this loss from the buyer.

It was held that, although the clause made no express
provision as to cash against documents on arrival, it was clear
from a proper construction of the clause that if the original
document was not available, then an alternative document was
to be presented promptly.

The seller tendering on 23 June was *not* prompt, but the buyer
had also led the seller to believe that he would not reject the
goods or documents. Therefore, the buyer could not later
re-assert the right where it would be unjust or unfair to do so.
The buyer had been inconsistent in his intent to reject the
goods and so had waived the seller's breach. The seller was
therefore entitled to payment of the contract price on tender
of the documents on 23 June.

In this case, therefore, the buyer had been in default and so was liable
for damages to the seller for failure to make payment on arrival of
the vessel. Although the documents had not been sighted at the time
of arrival of the vessel, the buyer waived his right to treat
non-production of alternative documents as a breach of condition by
not insisting upon them.

5.   Place of tender

In the past there has been uncertainty as to the place of tender
under a Cost Insurance Freight contract, but, since the case of *The
Albazero*, the position has become quite certain —

The Albazero (1975): Brandon L.J. stated that the place of tender is to be at the place of the buyer's business or residence. This seems to be the preferred location as to where the documents are to be tendered but other places may be specified in the contract.

Progress test 3

1. Why is it important for a buyer to scrutinise the documents under a Cost Insurance Freight contract? **(2)**

2. Under what circumstances may a seller tender documents even though there may be no goods available? **(3)**

3. When does the risk in the goods pass to a buyer under a Cost Insurance Freight contract? **(3)**

4. When should the slipper documents be tendered? **(4)**

5. What is the effect of a document being tendered out of time? **(4)**

6. What rule was established in the case of *The Albazero* (1975)? **(5)**

4
Functions of Bills of Lading

Introduction

1. The main functions of Bills of Lading

Bills of Lading were introduced in the sixteenth century, and are of the greatest importance in international sales transactions. They perform three main functions:

(a) the Bill of Lading represents a document of title;
(b) the Bill of Lading is evidence of the contract of carriage;
(c) the Bill of Lading acts as a receipt as to:
  (*i*) quantity;
  (*ii*) leading marks;
  (*iii*) apparent good order and condition of the goods.

These three functions will be examined in detail in this chapter.

The Bill of Lading as a document of title

2. Type of title conferred

The Bill of Lading is a document of *possessory title* but not *proprietary title*, i.e. it has both negative and positive components.

3. Positive components

In some circumstances, e.g. in a Cost Insurance Freight contract, possession of a Bill of Lading amounts to constructive possession of the goods themselves.

The Bill of Lading represents the goods in transit, so by transferring the Bill of Lading, one is effectively transferring the possession of the goods. In effect, the tendering of the Bill of Lading is the same as delivery of the goods —

Horst v. *Biddell Bros* (1912): A contract was drawn up for goods to be shipped from the United States to England. While the goods were aboard the ship, the seller tendered the Bill of Lading document to the buyer, demanding payment in return. The buyer refused to pay, contending that he would wait until the goods had actually arrived.

The contract did not specify *when* payment was to be made so s. 28 of the Sale of Goods Act 1979 was referred to which states:

Unless otherwise agreed, delivery of the goods and payment of the price are concurrent conditions: the seller must be ready and willing to give possession of the goods to the buyer in exchange for the price and the buyer must be ready and willing to pay the price in exchange for possession of the goods.

It was held that the handing over of the Bill of Lading to the buyer was equivalent to the handing over of possession of the goods. Therefore the buyer was obliged to meet the payment.

Thus, the Bill of Lading acts as a document of title to the goods, enabling the person to dispose of them while they are in transit. If a buyer gives the Bill of Lading to another buyer then the sub-buyer can claim the goods from the carrier on arrival.

4. Negative components

The converse of the above point is that only the person holding the Bill of Lading is entitled to claim delivery of the goods from the carrier —

Trucks & Spares v. *Maritime Agencies Ltd* (1951): An English seller sold a number of trucks and spares to a Canadian company (the buyer). The buyer went to claim delivery of the goods but had no Bill of Lading because, due to debts owed to the carrier, the seller did not receive one, i.e. the carrier had the Bill of Lading.

It was held by Lord Denning that the Bill of Lading must be produced to make a good title to the goods (i.e. to collect the goods).

5. Possible difficulties arising in the use of Bills of Lading

Difficulties may arise if:

(a) the Bill of Lading is destroyed;
(b) the Bill of Lading is lost;
(c) the Bill of Lading is not available for some other reason;

(d) perishable goods arrive before the buyer receives the Bill of Lading.

In such circumstances, the carrier may release the goods without a Bill of Lading on a letter of indemnity.

6. Letters of indemnity

A letter of indemnity is usually issued by a bank or other sound financial institution. This will indemnify the carrier against any liability that may arise and is regularly enforceable.

If the proper owner of the goods later produces the Bill of Lading and the carrier has already released them on a letter of indemnity, the carrier has committed the tort of conversion. However, the letter of indemnity means he will not suffer financially when sued by the rightful owner —

> *Sze Hai Tong Bank* v. *Rambler Cycle Co.* (1959): The seller contracted to sell bicycles to a company in Singapore (the buyer). The seller tendered the Bill of Lading to the buyer but he did not receive it before the arrival of the goods. None the less, the buyer went to collect the goods.
> The carrier delivered the goods but took the precaution of taking out an indemnity. The seller, who still had the Bill of Lading, came later to collect the goods because the buyer had refused to pay. However, the carrier had already given the goods to the buyer.
> It was held by Lord Denning that the contract is to deliver, on production of the Bill of Lading, to the person entitled under the Bill of Lading. This was not the case here so the carrier was liable under the tort of conversion.
> As a result, the seller sued the carrier and the carrier sued the buyer on the indemnity from the bank.

Therefore, if a carrier gives the goods to the wrong person, he or she may be sued for the tort of conversion but can then recover any losses under the indemnity. This is a common, legal, and reputable practice. The following case concerns the same legal point with some additional elements —

> *The Jag Dhir* (1986): Goods were released against an indemnity issued by a bank. The actual owner of the Bill of Lading sued the carrier under the tort of conversion. The issue in this case was the measure of the damages.
> It was held by the Privy Council that the carrier was liable and

should have paid for the full value of the goods at the date and destination of delivery.

The judgment in *The Jag Dhir* will apply even though the person claiming damages may not wholly own the goods. For example, a company may have contributed only 75 per cent of the cost of the Bill of Lading but the carrier will *still* have to pay the full value.

7. Passing of ownership under an international sales contract

Ownership passes at the same time as in a domestic sales contract, which is usually when the parties *intend* the property to pass. Generally this is when the Bill of Lading is handed over.

Possession always passes on transfer of the Bill of Lading but ownership or property only passes when the parties *intend* it to pass.

8. Transferring Bills of Lading

For the Bill of Lading to be transferable, it must be negotiable. Whether a Bill of Lading is negotiable or not is determined by the form in which it is written.

For instance, a Bill of Lading made out to a named consignee is *not* negotiable; e.g. Consignee Ken means the Bill of Lading is not transferable; it can only be given to Ken.

In contrast, a Bill of Lading made out to consignee, to shipper's order or bearer *is* negotiable and means the Bill of Lading may be transferred, e.g. to a sub-buyer; it does not have to go to a specified buyer.

Transferring a Bill of Lading, as we have seen, also means the transfer of all the contractual rights and liabilities involved, but only when *property in the goods* is passed rather than just their *possession*.

9. The *nemo* dat. rule

This rule is that the transferee cannot have a better title than the transferer, i.e. the predecessor transfers good title to a sub-buyer *only* if his or her own title is good.

10. Bills of Exchange — exceptions to the rule

Bills of Exchange are negotiable instruments. In comparison, Bills of Lading are not negotiable instruments as they only transfer possession and ownership cannot be transferred unless the parties intend it to pass. In this sense, a Bill of Lading is semi-negotiable.

11. The Bill of Lading as evidence of the contract of carriage

Sometimes the Bill of Lading is only evidence of the contract of carriage while, at other times, it is considered to contain the full terms of the contract of carriage.

12. Evidence of the contract between the shipper and the carrier

In the relationship between the original shipper and the carrier, the Bill of Lading will contain contractual terms but will not necessarily *be* the contract. This is logical because, in the vast majority of cases, the contract will have been made before the Bill of Lading is issued. In effect, it is very good *evidence* of the contract of carriage but is not the contract itself so can be rebutted.

The Bill of Lading is, therefore, only evidence of the terms of the contract and other evidence may be adduced to show that the actual contract contained different terms, so it is not conclusive evidence —

> *The Ardennes* (1951): A seller contracted for oranges to be sent to London. A verbal agreement was made between the seller and the carrier that the ship was to proceed *directly* to London in a bid to evade additional import duty that was due to be increased on 1 December. However, the Bill of Lading also had a printed liberty clause allowing the carrier to stop on the way. The carrier *did* stop on the way and thus did not get to London until 4 December. The seller sued the carrier for deviating from the route and the carrier relied on the written liberty clause.
>
> The issue of the case was what the actual terms of the contract were — were they those in the Bill of Lading or the oral agreements that were made.
>
> It was held by Lord Goddard that the Bill of Lading only constituted *evidence* of the contract of carriage and so other evidence could be admissible in rebuttal.
>
> The carrier was therefore in breach of the contract of carriage because he was bound by what was *actually agreed* (verbally) between the original contracting parties — the verbal agreement.

13. Evidence of the contract between the carrier and the buyer

In the relationship between the carrier and the buyer (third party) the Bill of Lading is central. If the Bill of Lading passes into the hands of a third party, he will be bound *only* by the terms set out in the Bill of Lading as it is presumed that he took it on those terms and did not know of any other terms agreed by the carrier and the original shipper —

Leduc v. *Ward* (1888): There was an oral agreement that the carrier could deviate and there was also a standard written liberty clause in the Bill of Lading.

It was held that the liberty clause contained the terms of the contract and that the oral agreement was inadmissible.

Because the ship had deviated some 1200 miles and the voyage was only meant to be a short one, the deviation was clearly outside the bounds of a reasonable interpretation of a standard liberty clause. Thus the deviation was unjustified and the carrier was held to be in breach of the contract of carriage and so liable.

14. An exception to the privity of contract rule

This is that third parties are not parties to the contract. Such an exception is due to s. 1 of the Bills of Lading Act 1855, which abrogates the privity doctrine between carrier and buyer. For s. 1 to operate, it is essential that property has been passed by the endorsee/consignee.

This section has caused difficulties when it comes to deciding exactly when the property passes.

15. The point at which property passes

The *San Nicholas* and the *Sevonian Team* cases both concern the passing of property and precisely when it occurs. It seems from these two cases that there is no need for simultaneous passing of property —

San Nicholas (1976): Lord Roskill pointed out that property does not pass by endorsement.

Sevonian Team (1983): Justice Lloyd held that property passed on the consignment and so s. 1 was fulfilled.

16. Proviso to s. 1 — property must pass

There are two views as to the meaning of this proviso:

(a) *The narrow view.* Property passes at the moment endorsement takes place or when the Bill of Lading is handed over, i.e. by reason of consignment or endorsement. The passing of property and consignment or endorsement must, therefore, be synchronised for s. 1 of the Bills of Lading Act 1855 to apply.

(b) *The wider view.* All that is necessary is that property passes and that there is endorsement of the Bill of Lading; there is no need for these to be performed simultaneously. The *San Nicholas* and *Sevonian Team* cases both support this wider view.

17. Non-s. 1 parties

Not everyone is a s. 1 party but the court may still imply that a contract of carriage on the same terms as in the Bill of Lading exists between the carrier and the holder of the Bill of Lading —

> *Brandt* v. *Liverpool Steam Navigation Co.* (1924): A merchant bank held a Bill of Lading as security for a loan it had made. The bank was not a s. 1 party but a pledgee.
> The goods arrived, but the loan had still not been repaid so the bank took possession of the goods and paid for the freight charges. After receiving the goods, the bank noticed that they were damaged and so wished to be compensated by the carrier. However, though the bank wanted to sue the carrier, it could not do so as it was not a s. 1 party, it was only a pledgee of the Bill of Lading and so did not satisfy the s. 1 Bills of Lading Act 1855 proviso.
> It was held that a contract of carriage could be implied between the carrier and the non-s. 1 party. The terms of the contract of carriage were those as expressed in the Bill of Lading and so the non-s. 1 party could sue the carrier on an *implied* contract of carriage.
> It was also held that a contract of carriage could be implied into the relationship between a carrier and a buyer and that the terms of the contract of carriage were fully contained in the terms of the delivery order.

If the circumstances of the case example had been different, would the outcome have been substantially different? For example:

(a) suppose freight charges had already been paid in advance, i.e. no freight charge was due, would it have made any difference to the existence of an implied contract;

(b) suppose there were no goods to deliver, would that have made any difference?

The answer to both these questions is no, as was concluded in *The Aramis* case —

> *The Aramis* (1987): The buyer presented two Bills of Lading for goods. In response to the first Bill of Lading, no cargo was received and, in response to the second, the cargo delivered

was well below the correct amount. The buyer wanted to sue the carrier.

It was held by Justice Evans that a contract could be inferred as it is possible to infer that the seller undertakes to deliver the goods according to the Bill of Lading directions by virtue of him accepting the Bill of Lading.

In this case, there was *partial* delivery of the goods, but what would have happened if there had been a *total failure* to deliver? No cases have yet tested this point.

18. Summary

Between the shipper or seller and the carrier, the Bill of Lading is always considered to be *evidence only* of the contract of carriage.

However, there are two situations in which the Bill of Lading is considered to contain the full terms of the contract of carriage:

(a) in the relationship between the carrier and the s. 1 party, the buyer;

(b) where a contract of carriage has been implied by the courts as existing between the carrier and the non-s. 1 party.

19. The Bill of Lading as a receipt

The Bill of Lading acknowledges receipt of the goods by the carrier. The Bill of Lading acts as a receipt for three things:

(a) quantity;

(b) leading marks;

(c) apparent good order and condition.

The Bill of Lading will acknowledge the *quantity of goods* put on board. These statements in the Bill of Lading are prima-facie evidence only and the carrier can rebut the evidence by proving that the goods stated were, in fact, not put on board or that the goods put on board were not as described, but this is not conclusive evidence —

Grant v. Norway (1851): This is an old case, but it is still relevant. Here the Bill of Lading stated that 12 bales of silk had been shipped on board, but, on arrival at its destination, the endorsee of the Bill of Lading discovered that there were none.

The carrier was able to prove that these 12 bales had never been put on board. It was held that the carrier was not liable for non-delivery.

It was also held that the shipmaster who signed the Bill of

Lading had actual authority to sign on behalf of the carrier only for goods actually shipped (loaded). By signing for non-existent goods, he was acting outside his actual authority and could not bind his principal. Therefore the *shipmaster* was liable for non-delivery, not the carrier.

Saudi Crown (1986): The shipmaster put the wrong date on a Bill of Lading. Was the carrier bound by this false dating of the Bill of Lading? He was held to be vicariously liable for his employee misrepresenting the date of shipment.

20. Authority of the shipmaster to act as a carrier's agent

The case examples in essence say that an agent has no authority to sign but a shipmaster does have apparent authority to put the date on a Bill of Lading. If he dates it incorrectly, his principal will be bound by it in contract or liable under tort for the misstatement — *see The Ocean Frost* (1986).

21. Responsibilities of an authorised agent

Actual and ostensible authority is now more developed. Section 3 of the Bill of Lading Act 1855 was enacted as a result of the *Grant* v. *Norway* (1851) (*see* 4:**19**) case. It is a conclusive evidence rule that, although it does not give rise to a cause of action, may be very helpful.

Section 3 does not give any right of action against the signatory of a Bill of Lading; it creates a statutory estoppel. It states that in the hand of the endorsee the Bill of Lading is conclusive evidence of '. . . shipment as against shipmaster or other person signing the same'.

Although the endorsee of the Bill of Lading for the incorrect quantity of goods may not, in Civil Law, be able to take action against the carrier, he may well be able to against the carrier's agent who signed the Bill of Lading —

Rasnoimport v. *Guthrie* (1966): The Bill of Lading said that 225 bales of rubber had been loaded and it was signed by the carrier's loading broker. However, only *90* bales had, in fact, been loaded. The endorsee of the Bill of Lading sued the carrier on two grounds:

(a) that s. 3 of the Bills of Lading Act 1855 gave rise to a substantial cause of action and
(b) the breach of warranty of authority.

Ground (a) did not succeed but ground (b) was successful.

It was held that the endorsee could recover damages for the missing bales from the loading brokers, the carrier's agents, in action for breach of warranty of authority.

Thus, actions against a carrier now are not worth pursuing as many will be judgment proof. However, the person who signed the Bill of Lading may be sued.

22. The extent of an agent's duty to accuracy

How thorough an inspection does a carrier need to conduct in order to justify the issuance of a clean Bill of Lading?

Because much loading of cargo is done at night, during storms and rain, etc., the opportunity for total and thorough inspection does not arise so only *reasonable inspection under the circumstances* is required —

> *Silver* v. *Ocean SS Co.* (1930): The plaintiff was the endorsee of two Bills of Lading that related to 18 000 tins of frozen eggs which had been shipped from China to London. The Bill of Lading said that they were shipped in apparent good order and condition.
> When the tins arrived in London, however, some had been damaged and these were rejected immediately by the endorsee. The other tins were still in apparent good order and condition and so the endorsee took these and stored them in his unrefrigerated warehouse. Many of them started to ooze.
> On close inspection it was found that the tins had tiny holes that had made no difference when the eggs were in their frozen state but obviously did when they had been defrosted.
> It was held by L.J. Scrutton that the carrier was liable in regard to the first batch, which were damaged, but not liable for the second batch that the buyer had stored in his warehouse because a reasonable inspection under the circumstances would nc. have disclosed the tiny holes, bearing in mind business conditions.

Thus, it seems that gross defects are expected to be spotted upon inspection but not microscopic ones. A written inspection under the circumstances is all that is required.

A clean Bill of Lading

23. When a clean Bill of Lading is issued that should not be

The usual formulation in a clean Bill of Lading is '. . . shipped in apparent good order and condition'. Sometimes a clean Bill of Lading is issued when it should not be. In Common Law action taken against a carrier for this improper insurance usually succeeds —

> *Compania* v. *Naviera* (1906): Timber was petrol stained before shipment, but the carrier still issued a clean Bill of Lading. The buyer claimed against the carrier. Here an estoppel arose and he was bound by the statement he had made in the Bill of Lading — that the timber had been shipped in apparent good order and condition — and so was liable as it was conclusive.

Sometimes an estoppel succeeds, sometimes it does not. It can be established if there is a clean Bill of Lading —

> *The Skarp* (1935): Timber had been shipped on the defendant's ship and a clean Bill of Lading had been issued, even though at the time of insurance the shipmaster knew the timber to be in bad condition. A clause in the contract stated that the endorsee could not reject the goods, he had to accept them and then arbitrate any dispute later. The endorsee sued the carrier. It was held that for a Common Law estoppel to arise:
>
> **(a)** some statement as to the existence of a contract would have to be made by the defendant to the plaintiff;
> **(b)** this statement has to be made with the intention that the plaintiff would act on the statement;
> **(c)** the plaintiff must, in fact, act on the statement.
>
> It was held that the first two points were established here but that the third had not been fulfilled. The buyer had only accepted the Bill of Lading because of the obligation to do so in the contract of sale.

> *Canadian Sugar Co.* v. *Canadian Steamships* (1947): The Bill of Lading related to a quantity of sugar. A clean Bill of Lading was issued but contained in the margin an endorsement: signed under guarantee to produce ship's clean receipt. The sugar was damaged. The plaintiff had the Bill of Lading and sued the carrier, claiming that the carrier was estoppel from saying that the sugar was shipped other than in apparent good order and condition.

24. Summary of s. 3 of the Bills of Lading Act 1855

If an agent acts *within* his or her authority, the principal is bound by those actions. However, if an agent acts *outside* his or her authority the principal is not bound.

If an agent has ostensible authority, the principal is bound by those actions but, if a third person suffers as a result, the third person can sue the agent for breach of warranty of authority under s. 3 of the Bills of Lading Act 1855. For example, if a shipmaster signs for unshipped goods and a third person suffers, the third person cannot sue the principal but may sue the shipmaster (or other person) who signed the Bill of Lading for unshipped goods. However, if the endorsee of the Bill of Lading *knows* the goods were never put on board he cannot sue the signer of the Bill of Lading.

If the shipmaster or other person signing the Bill of Lading can show that he was deceived into signing the Bill of Lading, then he may escape liability. However, this is difficult to prove as the shipmaster has a duty to check the goods he puts on board.

25. Leading marks

Goods usually have shipping marks put on them and these are also entered on the Bill of Lading. This is done for identification purposes and examples include distinguishing marks, code marks, symbols, etc. In Common Law, the carrier is entitled to show that goods shipped were marked differently than was noted in the Bill of Lading —

Parsons v. *NZ Shipping Co.* (1901): Some carcasses of frozen lamb were found on arrival to bear different marks to those given in the Bill of Lading. The marks only reflected details in the seller's storage system and did not relate to the quality or description of the goods.
It was held by L.J. Romer that the carrier could prove that the carcasses delivered were the ones actually loaded.

26. Apparent good order and condition

The shipmaster has the authority to report only as to the apparent good order and condition and *not* to the goods' inner condition and quality. Also, the Bill of Lading only relates to when the goods are put on board and does not cover any subsequent damage suffered by the goods —

The Galatia (1979): A cargo of sugar was loaded on board but, before the vessel sailed, a fire broke out and water was used to put the fire out. The result was that some 300 tons of the sugar was damaged. The spoiled sugar was discharged and the rest of the sugar was shipped to its destination.

The carrier issued two Bills of Lading: one that referred to good sugar shipped in apparent good order and condition and a second which referred to 300 tons of sugar shipped in apparent good order and condition but subsequently discharged because of fire and water damage.

The seller tendered the two Bills of Lading to the buyer who paid one of the Bills of Lading, but, as the second was not clean, refused to pay the seller.

It was held that *both* Bills of Lading were, in fact, clean. The second Bill of Lading only related to events that took place *after* the shipment, so it was still clean, i.e. the facts were correct when the goods were put on board. It was a Cost Insurance Freight contract and thus the seller's obligations ended on shipment. The buyer was therefore liable to pay for the sugar. Shipment occurs when goods are put on board ship — when they cross the ship's rails, not when the ship sails. Thus, if a Bill of Lading reads 'shipped in apparent good order and condition', it will be clean regardless of what it may say about damage suffered to the goods *after* shipment.

It was held that if one is qualifying a statement in the Bill of Lading as to apparent good order and condition, then it must be made obvious or else the court will say that it is still a clean Bill of Lading, e.g. it must be in small print or on the back. The language of the Bill of Lading read as a whole did not give rise to an estoppel because the statement as to apparent good order and condition was qualified by the receipt, on which was written, 'many bags stained, torn and resewn'.

27. Carriage of Goods by Sea Act 1971 (COGSA)

'Apparent good order and condition' creates an estoppel that a carrier is bound by that statement under this Act. Also, the carrier must issue a Bill of Lading on demand by the seller that indicates at least three descriptive elements, but there is no obligation for the carrier to do so unless the seller demands it. The three discipline elements are:

(a) leading marks necessary for identification of the goods;
(b) either the number of packages or pieces or the quantity or weight — *see Oricon Warren-Handels* (1967);
(c) the apparent order and condition of the goods.

Article III, Rule 4, COGSA 1971 covers the effect of making these statements; they become conclusive and binding on the carrier. The Bill of Lading is then prima-facie evidence of the receipt by the carrier of the goods described therein. However, proof to the contrary shall not be admissible when the Bill of Lading has been transferred to a third person acting in good faith. Rule 4, therefore, is a statutory estoppel and so the Common Law estoppel need not be looked at. There is no reference in Rule 4 to giving value or consideration and so really a donee could take advantage of Article III Rule 4.

Under Article III Rule 5, a buyer can sue a carrier, but the carrier will be indemnified by the seller. If a Bill of Lading does not exist, then there is no right of possession, but usually in such cases a letter of indemnity will be acceptable as it will indemnify the carrier for non- or misdelivery.

It is usual, therefore, for a buyer to sue a carrier and for the carrier to sue the seller on the indemnity. There are various types of indemnities, one of the more common ones was used in the following case —

> *Brown Jenkinson* v. *Percy Dalton* (1957): There was a contract for barrels of orange juice to be shipped. The barrels were old, just usable and leaking, but the seller told the carrier to, nevertheless, issue a clean Bill of Lading.
> The agent for the carrier issued a clean Bill of Lading after the shipper had agreed to indemnify the carrier's against any liability arising from the insurance of a clean Bill of Lading. Liability later arose. The carrier paid the buyer for the loss and then sued the seller on the contract of indemnity.
> It was held that the indemnity could not be enforced because it had all the elements of fraud and deceit.
> Indemnities may be acceptable in trivial matters that the buyer would not object to but not when there is a glaring defect as it will be considered fraudulent with regard to the buyer or whoever else relies on the statement in the Bill of Lading.

28. Good tender
A Bill of Lading must be of good tender. There are certain characteristics that a Bill of Lading must have to make it so.

The Bill of Lading must be in shipped form
This means that it must indicate that the goods have actually been

loaded on the ship and not just that they have been received by the carrier for shipment —

> *Diamond Alkali Export Corporation* v. *Bourgeois* (1921): The buyers were tendered with a Bill of Lading that said the carrier had received the goods in apparent good order and condition.
> It was held that the buyer could reject the documents tendered as a Cost Insurance Freight contract calls for a Bill of Lading to evidence shipment of the goods.

However, there have been other cases that have ruled that a receipt for shipment Bill of Lading is acceptable *if it is trade custom to do so*. Therefore, the custom of the trade could indicate an *opposite* response to that in the case above.

The Bill of Lading must be in a clean form
This means that it must not indicate an apparent defect in the goods on shipment.

> *Siat* v. *Tradax*: a clause in the contract read:
>
> In the event of any shortcoming in the documents tendered, the buyer must accept on the basis of the firm guarantee by Tradax.
>
> The Bill of Lading had a defect and the buyer rejected the documents.
> It was held that the clause was draconian as its effect was to cure any defects that may arise from the documents tendered.
> However, the clause was construed narrowly and it was concluded that the buyer could reject.
> Thus, although in principle one can try to cure any documentary tender by such clauses, the courts will construe such clauses restrictively.

The Bill of Lading must show the proper time and place on terms usual in the trade.
A Bill of Lading must only cover goods that are in the contract of sale; it must not cover goods in other contracts.
The Bill of Lading must be negotiable to enable the cargo to be dealt in whilst afloat, e.g. to order of X.
The Bill of Lading must give continuous documentary cover right up to the Cost Insurance Freight destination, provided by the carrier.
The Bill of Lading must be a through Bill of Lading
No ship will go straight from a contractual point to a Cost

Insurance Freight destination, therefore the goods are usually trans-shipped, which means that the goods are transferred from one ship to another at an intermediate port along the way, hence the need for a through Bill of Lading. Trans-shipment can be done in an emergency or be planned.

Through Bills of Lading are acceptable if they are proper. They must provide the carrier with a continuity of rights from the original point right up to the contractual destination and be proper and acceptable —

> *Hansson* v. *Hamel & Horley* (1922): The contract of sale was Cost Insurance Freight Yokohama in Japan from certain Norwegian ports. No ships went directly to the seller so it was arranged that the goods be carried from Norway to Hamburg and then from Hamburg to Yokohama.
> The carrier's agent signed a through Bill of Lading in Hamburg which stated that the goods were shipped in apparent good order and condition. Thus the Bill of Lading was not issued on shipment but from Hamburg Yokohama. The buyer rejected the documents.
> It was held that the buyer could reject the Bill of Lading because it did not cover the full route. The Bill of Lading issued from Hamburg was not a proper through Bill of Lading because it gave the buyer no protection for the first leg of the voyage from Norway to Hamburg.
> Also in a sale on Cost Insurance Freight terms, the contract of carriage must be procured *on shipment* and here the Bill of Lading was issued 13 days *after* shipment in a different country, so it could not be said to have been procured on shipment.

From this case it can be seen that the documents must be taken up or rejected promptly. Also, the carrier must ensure that the through Bill of Lading gives continuity of rights from the origin point to the Cost Insurance Freight destination. Lord Summer indicated, however, that this rule may not apply if there is a trade custom.

This case can be compared with another —

> *Meyer* v. *Aune* (1939): There was a Cost Insurance Freight contract for the sale of copra to be shipped from the Philippines Cost Insurance Freight Marcé.
> The copra was originally shipped from Sibu, a port outside the Philippines, then to the Philippines for trans-shipment to Marcé. The original Bill of Lading was surrendered at the

collecting port and a new one was issued that had been backdated to the original Bill of Lading from Sibu to Marcé. The buyer rejected the documents.

It was held that there had been good tender of the documents because it was the custom of the trade to give the buyer the Bill of Lading for just that part of the voyage.

J. Branson held that local custom was followed by the laws here. The carrier maintained a continuity of rights from the original place of shipment, Sibu, to Marcé because a proper Bill of Lading had been issued from the outset.

Thus, if there are any interruptions in the rights of the holder of the Bill of Lading, then it will not be good tender of the document.

Progress test 4

1. What is a Bill of Lading?   **(1)**

2. What are the main functions of a Bill of Lading and why is it so important?   **(1, 3)**

3. What is meant when a Bill of Lading is described as a document of title?   **(3)**

4. What are the positive and negative aspects of a Bill of Lading? **(3, 4)**

5. If a problem occurs with the Bill of Lading how may a carrier release the goods to the buyer?   **(6)**

6. When does the ownership and risk in the goods pass to the buyer?   **(7)**

7. What is a negotiable Bill of Lading?   **(8)**

8. What is the *nemo dat* rule?   **(9)**

9. List the things for which a Bill of Lading acts as a receipt.   **(19)**

10. What is a clean Bill of Lading?   **(23)**

11. What is the effect of s. 3 of the Bill of Lading Act 1855?
(21, 24)

12. What is needed for a Bill of Lading to be of good tender?   **(28)**

5

The COGSA 1971 and the Hague Visby Rules

Introduction

1. How the Act and Rules came into being

Until the eighteenth century, Bills of Lading did not contain exceptions, which meant that shipowners could not exempt themselves from liability if perils were to occur.

The situation has since changed with shipowners now relying heavily on widely used exclusion clauses within a Bill of Lading.

Eventually an international convention was introduced to attempt to strike a balance between the interests of shipowners and carriers. The meeting was held at The Hague in 1921 and finally adopted as the Hague Rules in 1922.

In due course trading nations met in 1924 and agreed to make these Hague Rules statutory. In Great Britain this was done via the Carriage of Goods by Sea Act 1924 (COGSA). This Act was later repealed, which meant that the Rules were then re-enacted. As a result, contracts for the carriage of goods by sea, under English law, are governed by the COGSA 1971, along with an international convention referred to as the Hague Visby Rules.

2. The Hamburg Rules

Despite the fact that the Hague Visby Rules were an improvement on the Hague Rules, many argue that they are mainly for the protection of the carrier. In 1978 a new convention was introduced, referred to as the The Hamburg Rules, but as yet these are not statutory in the UK. They are contained in a Schedule to the COGSA.

3. The Hague Visby Rules

The Hague Visby Rules have been made statutory by the 1971 COGSA and are therefore subject to the rules of statutory interpretation.

4. When the Rules apply

The Rules apply to Bills of Lading that relate to the carriage of goods between ports. This happens in three main situations:

(a) when the Bill of Lading is issued in a state that is a party to the convention;

(b) if the carriage is from a port in a contracting state;

(c) when the contract provides by a clause that the Rules are to apply.

The carrier can therefore escape the COGSA and the Rules if the contract with the shipper does not provide that a Bill of Lading is to be issued. A non-negotiable receipt may be issued instead by cross-channel operators — *see Browner International Transport Ltd* v. *Monarch SS Co. Ltd* (1989). However, such non-negotiable receipts may still be caught if they have a clause to the effect that it is to be treated '... as if the receipt were a Bill of Lading'. This is in line with s. 1(b)(b) of COGSA 1971.

Article III(8) of the Rules makes it clear that a carrier cannot exclude liability for duties imposed —

The Morviken (1983): This case concerned a situation in which a clause in the Bill of Lading adopted a legal system that had not incorporated the enlarged liability of the carrier under the Rules. The House of Lords held that the choice of law in favour of Netherlands law was ineffective under article III(8).

Duties under the Hague Visby Rules

5. Due diligence

In Common Law there is an absolute obligation that the carrier is to provide a seaworthy ship. However, under article III, rule 1 of the Rules, this obligation has been relaxed to one of due diligence. Although it is usually the carrier who is affected by rule 1 it is not restricted to carriers —

Riverstone Meat Co. v. *Lancashire Shipping Co.* (1961): The carriers had appointed a reputable and competent firm of repairers, they were negligent in failing to replace storm-value covers. It was held that despite such negligence the carrier was liable under article III, rule 1 for failing to exercise due diligence as such a duty can be delegated to another party.

This duty under article III, rule 1 applies from the time loading of the ship begins straight through to when the voyage begins, but does not extend to the actual voyage —

> *The Makedonia* (1962): Here the plaintiffs shipped timber on board a vessel for a voyage to the UK. The ship broke down in mid-ocean and had to take salvage assistance. The plaintiffs tried to recover the share of the salvage award that they had to pay. J. Hewson held that the obligation to exercise due diligence before and at the beginning of the voyage had been fulfilled.

The carrier's obligation of due diligence under article III, rule 1 would include the following:

(a) the ship must be fit to receive the cargo under article III, rule 1(c), but also to carry and to be able to deliver it to its destination — *see The Good Friend* (1984);

(b) the ship must be fit in its design, structure, condition and equipment to cope with the ordinary perils of the voyage;

(c) the ship must have competent and sufficient crew and the shipmaster must also be aware of how to run the ship —

> *Standard Oil Co. of NY* v. *Clan Line Steamers* (1924): The vessel was held to be unseaworthy because the shipmaster had not been furnished with instructions as to special dangers that her design involved. The ship was lost because the shipmaster, being uninstructed, made a manoeuvre that caused her to capsize. He would not have done so had he been given correct instructions. Nevertheless, Lord Atkinson held that the shipmaster was responsible as his handling of the ship amounted to gross and flagrant mismanagement.

6. Whether or not a ship is seaworthy

If a carrier is to be sued for not exercising due diligence, then it must be shown that the ship was unseaworthy and that there was a causal link between this and the loss or damage. This point has been reinforced by Mr Justice McNair in *Ministry of Food* v. *Reardon-Smith Line Ltd* (1951). He said that the burden of proving that the loss was caused by unseaworthiness was upon the goods owner.

It is therefore the cargo owner who has the burden of proof under article III, rule 1.

7. Article III, rule 2

Under article III, rule 2, a carrier has no choice but to properly and carefully load, stow, carry, keep, care for and discharge the goods, otherwise there will be breach of contract.

In order to do this, a system must be adopted that is sound in light of all the knowledge that the carrier has, or ought to have, about the nature of the goods. This task should not be delegated.

8. Burden of proof

The burden of proof is, initially, on the cargo owner to establish that the goods have not arrived at their destination or that they arrived in a damaged condition. There is no need to prove negligence.

Once this is done it is then the carrier who has to prove that the cause of the damage falls within one of the expected perils, e.g. peril of the sea, ship's structure, act of God, war —

The Torenia (1983): The carrier was unable to prove that the loss incurred was due to the ship's latent defect and was, therefore, fully liable for the loss.

A good example of how this operates can be seen in *Phillips Petroleum Co.* v. *Cabaneli Naviera SA* (1990).

9. Article III, rule 3

Under article III, rule 3, the carrier must issue a Bill of Lading on demand by the seller indicating at least three descriptive elements. However, there is no obligation for the carrier to do this unless the seller demands it.

The elements are:

(a) leading marks necessary for identification of the goods;
(b) either the number of packages or pieces or the quantity or weight;
(c) the apparent order and condition of the goods.

10. Article III, rule 4 — statutory estoppel created

Article III, rule 4 creates a statutory estoppel. It covers the effect of making the statements in article III, rule 3 (above). They become binding and conclusive on the carrier. The Bill of Lading is then prima-facie evidence of the receipt by the carrier of the goods described. However, proof to the contrary shall not be admissible when the Bill of Lading has been transferred to a third party acting in good faith.

11. Article III, rule 5 — indemnities

Article III, rule 5 states, in effect, that if a Bill of Lading does not exist, then there is no right of possession, but a letter of indemnity will be acceptable as it will indemnify the carrier for non- or mis-delivery. Therefore, a buyer will sue the carrier and the carrier will sue the shipper on the indemnity, of which there are many types — see *Brown Jenkinson* v. *Percy Dalton* (1957) (4:**27**). Thus, indemnities may be acceptable in trivial matters that the buyer will not object to but not when there is a glaring defect as this will be regarded as fraud with regard to the buyer or whoever relies on the statement in the Bill of Lading.

Progress test 5

1.   Why are the Hague Visby Rules an improvement on the Hague Rules?   **(1, 2)**

2.   When do the Hague Visby Rules apply?   **(4)**

3.   How may a carrier escape these Rules?   **(4)**

4.   What is the effect of Article III (8) of the rules?   **(4)**

5.   What are the main duties of the carrier under the Hague Visby Rules?   **(5)**

6.   What is the burden of proof?   **(8)**

7.   What is the effect of Article III, Rule 3?   **(9)**

8.   What is the effect of Article III, Rules 4 and 5?   **(10, 11)**

6
Delivery orders

Introduction

1. Why delivery orders are used

Common Law requires that the seller tender a Bill of Lading, but sometimes this may not be possible. This usually happens when there is a bulk shipment that is to be dealt with in a piecemeal fashion as the elements are broken down and sold in small quantities to a number of buyers. For example: the buyer buys 1000 tons of corn to resell in smaller lots to several sub-buyers. In such circumstances the Bill of Lading could not be given to only *one* buyer because there will be other sub-buyers. Thus, the practice of having a documentation substitution clause for a Bill of Lading has developed. This substitution takes the form of a delivery order, which can be given to each individual buyer for his particular quantity of goods.

Lord Denning in *Colin & Shield* v. *Weddel* (1952) stated that 'Cost Insurance Freight contracts are often modified to allow a delivery order to be made instead of a Bill of Lading'.

The nature of delivery orders

2. When a delivery order is issued

A delivery order is issued in either of the following instances after the issuance of a Bill of Lading:

(a) *On surrender of the Bill of Lading by the seller*. This is then called a delivery warrant. The seller will surrender the Bill of Lading to the carrier and then the carrier will issue it, promising to deliver the goods in the quantities called for by the seller to various named parties.

(b) *When there is an order or instruction from the seller to the carrier to deliver in various amounts to various parties*. The carrier will then attorn, i.e. will acknowledge that he (the carrier) is holding the goods for the parties named in the order/instruction.

In both these cases of promise or attornment, the carrier says that he will deliver.

3. Shipped delivery orders

A shipped delivery order is the only type of delivery order that can be valid tender under a substitution clause in a Cost Insurance Freight contract. A shipped delivery order contains some undertaking on the part of the carrier, who has the goods in his possession, that he will deliver them to the holder of the delivery order according to the seller's order or instruction. The holder of a delivery order cannot claim under s. 1 of the Bills of Lading Act 1855, as could a Cost Insurance Freight Bill of Lading holder, and so the rights are not as unassailable as under a Bill of Lading.

Once a Bill of Lading is handed over, it will represent constructive possession of the goods because the Bill of Lading is a document of title, but a delivery order is *not* a document of title so its transfer does not give constructive possession of the goods. There must be attornment first to gain constructive possession of the goods.

A buyer can reject any other delivery order that is not a shipped delivery order as it will not be compatible with the Cost Insurance Freight contract. Many types of documents have been tendered that are not delivery orders —

> *Comptoir d'Achat* v. *Luis de Ridder* (1949): In this case there was an Arrival contract (not Cost Insurance Freight) because the documents did not entitle the buyer to collect the goods from the ship, only from the warehouse. The seller's agent instructed another seller's agent, who was named in the contractual destination, to deliver the goods to the buyer. It was held that this form of delivery order was unacceptable under a Cost Insurance Freight contract as it gave no rights against the carrier.

> *Colin & Shield* v. *Weddel* (1952): The document was one issued by the seller, instructing the master porter of the Hydebirth in Liverpool the Cost Insurance Freight destination and to deliver goods to the order of the buyer. There was an instruction to an official of a port authority in Liverpool but it

had no connection with the ship. It was held that it was not a satisfactory delivery order.

Singleton L.J. in the case said that the delivery order must be issued by someone who has the authority to do so.

4. Conditions attached to delivery orders

Unless it appears to the contrary, the general conditions of a Cost Insurance Freight sale are not waived by the substitution of a delivery order for a Bill of Lading — see Ginzberg v. Barrow Haematite (1966). (In summary, a delivery order was used to expedite delivery, but this was held not to affect rights of an unpaid seller under a Cost Insurance Freight contract) —

Margarine Union v. Cambay Prince (1967): Otherwise known as 'The Wear Breeze', delivery orders were not permitted under the contract but were accepted by the Cost Insurance Freight buyer. The issue was whether the buyer could succeed in a claim against the carrier whose negligence in failing to fumigate the vessel caused damage to a consignment of copra. It was held that the buyer could not take such action as the delivery order conferred no propriety to the copra in question (this was needed to have an action in tort against the carrier). It was immaterial that the risk in the copra had passed.

Where the delivery order is issued by the carrier and held to incorporate the terms of any Bill of Lading issued in respect of the cargo in question, then the holder of the delivery order can recover for breach of contract —

Cremer v. General Carriers (1974): A quantity of tapioca roots were bought on Cost Insurance Freight terms from a seller in Thailand reselling a portion to a second plaintiff to whom delivery orders incorporating the terms of the Bill of Lading were issued. Although the roots were not dry, a clean Bill of Lading was issued by the shipmaster.

Kerr J. held in the case that there was a contract between the seller and the second plaintiff, although before delivery they were not owners of any part of the undivided bulk of the cargo, and so the second plaintiff could sue the seller for breach of contract. The seller was estoppel from relying pre-shipment condition of the goods because they had issued a clean Bill of Lading.

Krohn v. Thegra (1975): There was a contract for sale of goods

Cost Insurance Freight Rotterdam. Payment was to be against the documents. The documents were to include a full set of on board Bill of Lading and/or ship's delivery order and/or other delivery order in negotiable and transferable form, i.e. the seller had various methods of performance.

From these cases it can be deduced that, although a contract may be called Cost Insurance Freight, one cannot be really sure what it is until the seller performs because he retains the option by virtue of possession of the Cost Insurance Freight or Arrival contract.

5. Title

Delivery orders are not documents of title in the same sense that Bills of Lading are. There are different definitions of 'document of title' under the Sale of Goods Act 1979.

A seller is in possession of the goods if he can pass on property to a third party by virtue of s. 24 of the Sale of Goods Act 1979, which means that he can sell goods to a sub-buyer.

Section 16 of the Sale of Goods Act states that the 'document of title includes a Bill of Lading document, warrants or orders for the delivery of goods or any other document used in the ordinary course of business as proof of the possession or control of goods or authorising or purporting to authorise either by endorsement or by delivery the possessor of the document to transfer or receive goods thereby represented'.

It can be seen, therefore, that the document of title has a wider meaning under the Act as it includes delivery orders, as opposed to Common Law, which restricts it to a Bill of Lading only.

Progress test 6

1. What is a delivery order and when does it get used?   **(1, 2)**

2. Why is a shipped delivery order so important?   **(3)**

3. Why is a delivery order not a document of title in the same way that a Bill of Lading is?   **(5)**

7
The insurance document

What is required

1. The type of insurance cover required

The law as to the type of insurance cover required under a Cost Insurance Freight contract seems to follow the custom of the trade. There are different types of marine insurance policies, although the main ones latterly are the Institute Cargo Clauses, A, B and C. The others are:

(a) with average policy (WA);
(b) free from particular average policy (FPA), which tend to be lesser policies that are tied in with particular named risks causing a loss;
(c) all risk policy (ARP), which covers all risks subject to exceptions.

At one time, only a free from particular average policy was required to be tendered, but there were also situations where other policies had to be tendered.

2. Amount of coverage needed

Traditional UK law does not offer any pointers regarding the coverage needed because all that is required is that the insurance be *for the value of the goods at the time and place of shipment*. This is usually *less* than the Cost Insurance Freight price as it does not include the freight and insurance elements.

However, an improvement can be found where incoterms have been incorporated, because, under incoterms, the seller's obligation calls for insurance for the full Cost Insurance Freight price, plus 10 per cent to reflect the average profit expectation of the buyer. This is to be expressed in the same currency as that in which payment is to be made under the contract.

3. Documents that must be tendered

Under Common Law, the position is clearly that only an

insurance policy can be tendered under a Cost Insurance Freight contract — no lesser documents will be acceptable. However, the need may arise for more than one insurance policy. For example, the seller selling to the buyer, who then sells to a sub-buyer who sells on to another sub-buyer in a chain contract.

In such circumstances, one may have a substitution clause in the contract to this effect. This substitute is called an insurance certificate.

It is usual for contracts to have substitution clauses for both the Bill of Lading and the insurance policy. For example, one can substitute a Bill of Lading for a delivery order or an insurance policy can be substituted for an insurance certificate.

4. The reasons for having documentary substitution clauses in insurance
These are as follows:

(a) *Speed.* An insurance certificate will get to the buyer sooner than the insurance policy itself. Also if cash is to be paid against documents, then the seller can be paid earlier. If cash is to be paid against documents, then the seller can be paid sooner.

(b) *Umbrella cover.* If a regular shipper is used then he will not place the insurance singly for each arrangement, i.e. facilitate insurance. Instead, he can have an umbrella cover arrangement, provided through the insurance certificate via a floating, or open, cover policy.

5. The point to which the insurance is to be provided
The geographical extent of insurance coverage is identical to the Cost Insurance Freight destination, whether somewhere abroad or evident —

> *Lindon* v. *White & Meacham* (1975): In this case there was a sale of Danish pullovers Cost Insurance Freight Ealing. However, the goods were misdirected to the buyer's office in the city of London. The buyers left the goods outside and asked the seller to redeliver them to Ealing. In the meantime, someone stole the goods. The buyer, therefore, sued the seller as the insurance document tendered only covered the goods to London, it did not cover them all the way to Ealing.
> It was held in the case that it was not a good tender as the goods should have been covered right up to Ealing. The seller had not therefore fulfilled his Cost Insurance Freight obligations completely under the contract.

The insurance cover taken out must, therefore, comply with the contract; if it does not say, then it must correspond with the custom of the trade.

6. What amount do you cover the goods for?

To decide this one must look at the terms of the contract. If it does not specify, then one must insure for their reasonable value at the place of shipment. This is not satisfactory to the buyer as the cargo will be worth more on arrival at the destination and so he must arrange in the contract for a higher cover.

7. Types of loss

It used to be important to know whether a loss was a total loss or a partial loss because, under the old free from particular average policy and with average policies, some or all forms of partial loss would not be covered. Now, however, the distinction between total and partial loss is irrelevant in the Institute Cargo Clause. Total loss of *any* package lost overboard or dropped while loading on to, or unloading from, vessel or craft is *not* covered by the Institute Cargo Clause policy.

8. Total loss

This can be one of two types — actual or constructive:

(a) *Actual total loss*. This is defined in s. 57 of the Marine Insurance Act 1906. It states that '... where the shipmaster insured is destroyed, or so damaged as to cease to be a thing of the kind insured, or where the assured is irretrievably deprived thereof, there is an actual total loss, ... or so damaged as to cease ...' comes from a carriage case —

> *Asfor* v. *Blundell* (1896): A shipment of dates had been carried under a Bill of Lading that made freight payable on delivery. The ship sailed for a few days and was then reloaded and eventually pulled into a London dock.
> The cargo of dates looked like dates and had some commercial value for distillation purposes but were no longer merchantable as dates. The shipmaster therefore has ceased to be a thing of the kind insured and so the carrier was not entitled to payment of the freight.

(b) *Constructive total loss*. Section 61 of the Marine Insurance Act 1906 states that a constructive total loss occurs when the ship is abandoned because its actual total loss seems unavoidable or because it could not be preserved from an actual total loss without incurring expenditure that would have exceeded its value.

Section 61 goes on to state that where there is a constructive total loss, the assured may either treat the loss as a partial loss or abandon the shipmaster insured to the insurer and treat the loss as if it were an actual total loss.

For the assured to claim for a constructive total loss, a notice of abandonment must be given to the insurer, as stipulated in s. 62. There is no standard form to be used when giving a notice of abandonment as long as it is clear and unconditional. However, the insurer does not have to accept the notice of abandonment (s. 62(b)) If he does accept the notice of abandonment, then it is irrevocable. The acceptance conclusively admits liability for the loss and that he will pay a total loss claim —

Boon & Chean (1975): A Privy Council decision, here the plaintiffs were owners of 668 steel pipes that were insured on free from particular average policy terms.
They were being carried by a barge that was pulled by a tug. During the voyage, the barge was damaged by one of the perils of the seas. The result was that all except 12 of the pipes were lost overside and sank. The remaining 12 were in a damaged condition. The plaintiffs claimed that:
  (*i*) the cargo was a *constructive total loss* and
  (*ii*) the cargo was an *actual total loss* by application of the *deminius* principle.
The courts held that the test is whether the cost of recovering, reconditioning and forwarding the goods to the destination would exceed their value on arrival. Applying this test, the critics said that the expenses were not greater than the value of the remaining pipes and so it was not a constructive total loss. The *deminius* principle could not be applied to generate an actual total loss and, thus, there could be no claim under the free from particular average policy.

The Bantun (1982): This was a judicial arbitration and Staughton J. was the sole arbitrator. The ship was a specialised cement carrier. In September 1980, the ship was carrying cement from Montbassah to an Iraqi port. In December 1980 the ship arrived in the Iraqi port when Iraq was invaded by Iran. The shipmaster was told that the ship could not sail as all vessels had been prohibited from leaving the port so the shipmaster and crew evacuated the ship. On 22 December

1980, a skeleton crew returned to live on board the ship. The ship was not damaged during this time, nor had the authorities asserted any rights, the ship was simply unable to sail.

In October 1981, the shipowner gave a notice of abandonment to the insurers for a constructive total loss by reason of the perils insured against. The owner's claim was based on s. 60 of the Marine Insurance Act 1906, contending that there was detention of the ship caused by a peril insured against.

The court held that this was true. There was no necessity to show physical force as the instruction not to sail was enough. The court also held that the owner had been deprived of possession of the ship. In addition, it was held to be unlikely that the owners could recover the vessel within a right time. Right time is computed not from the original detention but from the time of giving the notice of abandonment to the insurers. Right time was therefore 12 months in this case.

Other issues that sometimes arise in marine insurance claims are general average and salvage charges, which include suing and labour.

9.   General average

Under the law of carriage, if some act is intentionally done to prevent a disaster or to mitigate a loss that would have put the entire interest at risk and it meant some real cost or sacrifice and there was objective danger, then that is a general average act. There is a general average act when any extraordinary sacrifice or expenditure is voluntarily and reasonably made or incurred in time of peril for the purpose of preserving the property imperilled in the common adventure — see s. 66(2) of the Marine Insurance Act 1906. An example of a general average sacrifice would be throwing cargo overboard to lighten the ship in order to save it and the crew.

If the party claiming the general average act has contributed in some way to bringing about the situation of danger then he is prevented from succeeding with the claim. There is no liability for any general average loss or contribution where the loss was *not* incurred for the purpose of avoiding or in connection with the avoidance of a peril insured against — see s. 66(B) of the Marine Insurance Act 1906.

However, s. 66(B) has been contracted out of by Clause 2 of the Institute Cargo Clauses. Clause 2 states that insurance covers general average acts incurred to avoid, or in connection with avoidance of, loss from *any cause* except those excluded in salvage charges.

Section 62(2) states that this means the charges are recoverable under maritime law by a salvor independently of contract. Where there has been salvage activity undertaken under a contract there will be salvage charges in return if it is to prevent a peril insured against.

Section 65 has also been contracted out by Clause 2 of the Institute Cargo Clauses (*ante*).

Progress test 7

1. What are the meanings of WA, FPA and ARP?   (1)

2. What amount of insurance cover is required for goods?   (2, 5)

3. What is a certificate of insurance and when would it be used? (3, 4)

4. What is the difference between total and partial loss?   (7, 8)

5. What is a general average act?   (9)

8
Notice of appropriation

Introduction

1. What a notice of appropriation is

A notice of appropriation is not part of the shipping documents. It is a communication from the seller to the buyer (sometimes by telephone, but usually by telex or fax) informing the buyer that the goods have been shipped. It is a preliminary communication that the buyer will receive before the actual shipping documents. This advance statement gives particulars of the shipment, when and on what vessel the goods have been shipped, so that the buyer can enter into sub-contracts knowing that he can perform those Cost Insurance Freight contracts as the goods have been appropriated to him.

Such a notice of appropriation is not required under Common Law but under modern Grain and Feed Trade Association and Federation of Oils, Seeds and Fats Association and other trade association contracts they have frequently been requested.

The legal effect of giving a notice of appropriation

2. The legal effect

Section 16 of the Sale of Goods Act 1979 states that where there is a contract for the sale of unascertained goods, no property in the goods is transferred to the buyer unless and until the goods are ascertained. This therefore means that at the time of contracting all goods are either *specific* (ascertainable) or *unascertainable* (unidentifiable). For the property in the goods to be passed, the goods must first be ascertainable. A notice of appropriation can ascertain goods and permit property to pass thereafter.

Examples

(1) If there is a Cost Insurance Freight contract for 5000 tonnes of wheat and this has been shipped to the buyer in a ship that can only hold 5000 tonnes, the giving of a notice of appropriation will ascertain the goods, thereby overcoming the preliminary hurdle of passing property in those goods.

(2) If, however, the 5000 tonnes contract is being performed with other contracts, e.g. the ship is also carrying another 20 000 tonnes of goods to the Cost Insurance Freight destination, the giving of a notice of appropriation will not be able to ascertain the goods because, with such bulk, the goods cannot be ascertained until physically separated from the other goods on arrival. So here s. 16 of the Sale of Goods Act 1979 could *not* be fulfilled by giving a notice of appropriation.

Thus a notice of appropriation can ascertain goods and fulfil s. 16 of the Sale of Goods Act 1979 as it clarifies the terms of a contract, making the sale of unascertained goods a sale of specific goods. However, if the terms of the contract of sale have been added then the goods cannot be ascertained.

---

3. Revocation

The giving of a notice of appropriation cannot, unless the contract otherwise provides, be revoked by the seller, even if the seller has declared the wrong ship by mistake —

Grain Union SA Antwerp v. *Hans Larsen*: One of the conditions of the contract was that a notice of appropriation with the ship's name, date of the Bill of Lading and approximate quantity loaded was to be posted to the buyer within three days or telegraphed within seven days from the date of the Bill of Lading and a valid notice of appropriation once given was not to be withdrawn.

The seller received information that a cargo to fulfil the contract had been loaded onto the 'Triton' but a clerk employed by the seller sent a notice of appropriation to the buyer saying that the goods had been shipped on the 'Iris'. The seller later corrected the notice of appropriation but the buyer refused to accept the cargo on the ground that the notice giving the name of the 'Iris' was a valid notice of appropriation within the meaning of the contract and could not be withdrawn.

Branson J. held in the case that the buyer could reject. He stated that, '. . . unless it can be shown that it is not a valid notice of appropriation then it cannot be withdrawn . . . it seems to me that a notice of appropriation which contains all the essentials, the ship's name, the date of the Bill of Lading and the approximate quantity of the goods on board, if all these three elements are in conformity with the contract, is a valid Notice of Appropriation'.

Here the contract was for unascertainable goods by description but the notice of appropriation changed the terms of the contract, making it for goods shipped on board the 'Iris' i.e. was specific. The notice of appropriation was valid and so the seller could not amend or withdraw otherwise the seller would be in breach of his obligations.

4.   Unconditional appropriation

Appropriation is not to be confused with s. 18(5) of the Sale of Goods Act 1979, which relates to unconditional appropriation, which is one of the rules that relate to the passing of property.

Under s. 18(5)(1) of the Act, where there is a contract for the sale of unascertained or future goods by description and the goods of that description are in a deliverable state and are unconditionally appropriated to the contract, either by the seller with the assent of the buyer or by the buyer with the assent of the seller, the property in the goods then passes to the buyer. The assent may be expressed or implied and may be given either before or after the appropriation is made.

Section 18(5)(2) goes on to state '. . . does not reserve the right of disposal, he is to be taken to have unconditionally appropriated the goods to the contract . . .'.

Section 18(5)(2) has been interpreted to mean loss of the power of disposal over the goods. However, the giving of a notice of appropriation does not take away the power to dispose of the goods once the shipping documents are retained —

Krohn v. *Toepfer* (1975): There was a contract Cost Insurance Freight Hamburg for tapioca pellets to be sold on the basis of Grain and Feed Trade Association form 100.

Clause 10 in the contract stated that a notice of appropriation was to be given. On 1 February the seller sent the buyer a telex saying that the goods were shipped on 19 January on a ship called the 'Vladamir' (or better name).

On 1 February the buyer replied and said that he rejected the notice of appropriation as no ship by that name had been loaded on 19 January. The seller then amended the notice of appropriation and said that a ship called the 'Vladamir Ilych' was carrying the goods. The buyer still rejected and said 'or better name' probably referred to mistakes or errors. It was held, with Donaldson J. giving the main judgment, that '. . . an appropriation that comes later. Accordingly, validity depends on form and timing and not upon substance or factual accuracy. The appropriation was made within the proper time and not defective in form. At first sight it might be thought that to specify the 'Vladamir' (or better name) deprived the appropriation of its essential certainty, but it appears that the addition of these words (or better name) had been accepted in that trade for over forty years . . . They have been held to have no further effect than the limited right to correct errors in transmission and accordingly, the appropriation was valid'. The buyer was also unsuccessful in his alternative argument that he could accept the notice of appropriation as an anticipatory breach on the grounds that the seller could not perform as contracted as the goods had been shipped on the 'Vladamir Ilych' and not on the 'Vladamir'. In this case, trade practice was introduced to cover the shortcomings and to correct the notice of appropriation. In this area, the law does follow trade practice quite strictly.

A notice of appropriation has elements of contract, not performance and so the notice of appropriation is a matter of contractual completion, rather than one of performance.

5. Completion and performance

If a notice of appropriation is required but is not given or if it is not given in time, then the contract will be breached. In such circumstances, should litigation arise, then the notice of appropriation will be a matter of performance. In this respect, therefore, a notice of appropriation can be seen as a matter of contractual completion as well as one of performance —

Tradax v. *André* (1976): Tradax sold soya bean meal to André Cost Insurance Freight Rotterdam. The shipment period was April 1973 on a Grain and Feed Trade Association 100 form. The Bill of Lading was dated 6 April. On 6 May, the seller (not the original shippers) received a notice of appropriation that was passed on to the buyer on 17 May. The buyer rejected it. On 18 May, the seller replied, asking the buyer to receive but the buyer said that the notice of appropriation was 42 days late and so the seller would have to prove that he was part of a string contract, but he could not and so he was in default. In the Grain and Feed Trade Association form 100 there is a clause that says that a notice of appropriation is to be given within 10 days of the shipment of the goods. However, if the seller is in a string and receives the notice of appropriation before X date and then gives notice on the same day it will be deemed that he has complied with the clause. Even if the notice of appropriation is received after X date and notice is given the following day, then the seller will still be deemed to be in compliance with the 10-day rule.

In this case, however, the notice of appropriation was given 42 days after the shipment date and so the seller could only establish that it was a valid notice of appropriation by proving the string. In the litigation that arose, Donaldson J. held that unless the provisions of Clause 10 were strictly complied with, then a notice of appropriation given outside the 10-day period would be invalid.

He further held that this strict compliance included the shipper or subsequent sellers. Thus the seller has to prove that not only him but also every other party on in the string had dispatched the notice of appropriation within the 10-day provision. This is very difficult because, although he may be able to show this for himself, a string may include as many as 40-50 parties and so for him to establish that they were *all* within the 10-day rule is almost impossible.

Thus, here the seller was in breach, the date of default being 10 May when the 10-day rule ended.

Krohn v. *Toepfer* (1975): Failure to give a valid notice of appropriation was a breach of contract but in *Tradax* v. *André* (1976) (8:5) it was breach of performance. A seller cannot therefore validate a late notice *vis-à-vis* his buyer by dispatching it promptly.

A valid notice of appropriation cannot be withdrawn except with the buyer's consent, and, if the buyer rejects the first notice as being invalid and stale, then the seller is free to make a new notice of appropriation and tender different goods within the time permitted by the contract —

Getreide v. *Itoh* (1979): There was a contract for soya beans, based on a Federation of Oils, Seeds and Fats Association form 24, Cost Insurance Freight Rotterdam. The Federation of Oils, Seeds and Fats Association form 24 contains a clause to the effect that a notice of appropriation is to be dispatched by the first seller not later than seven days after shipment and that subsequent sellers are to dispatch notices within a reasonable time.

The seller, who was not the original shipper, received notice of dispatch on 10 June. On 15 June they tendered notice to the buyer, but the buyer rejected the notice as being outside the time limit. On 23 June, the seller tendered a new notice of appropriation that related to different goods, which were shipped on 17 June. The buyer also rejected this second notice of appropriation, saying that the seller's first notice was valid, although out of time, and so it could not be withdrawn for a new one without the buyer's consent.

It was held in the case that the notice of appropriation only served to appropriate goods to the contract and so modified the rights of the parties. Therefore the seller was free to make a new notice of appropriation because the first notice of appropriation was out of time and so invalid and ineffective, the new notice of appropriation avoided any breach.

It can be concluded that if a seller gives a valid notice of appropriation that is inaccurate, he will be stuck with it *unless* the contract entitles any amendment of such inaccuracies. However, if a new one is issued, then it will avoid any breach. Once a valid, in time notice of appropriation is given, the seller cannot withdraw or amend it, even if he cannot perform the contract.

6.   Time limits

The following case illustrates what the position is when no time limit has been set for giving a notice of appropriation.

The Post Chaser (1981): The seller sold the buyer some palm oil Cost Insurance Freight Rotterdam and the contract of sale provided that the notice of appropriation be made to the buyer as soon as possible after the vessel had set sail.

On 16 December 1974, the seller received a notice of appropriation in respect of palm oil shipped on 6 December. The seller did not re-tender the notice of appropriation to the buyer until 10 January 1975, which was late. In the meantime, the buyer had concluded a sub-sale and further sub-sales after this. On 13 January a notice of appropriation was passed along the string that was later rejected by a sub-buyer on 14 January. On 20 January the original buyer telexed the seller, asking for documents to be tendered to the sub-buyer and this was done on the same day. On 21 January, the sub-buyer rejected the

notice. Then, on 22 January, the seller resold the palm oil for
£460 per ton when the original contract between the seller
and the buyer was for £792 per ton. The seller sued the buyer
for the difference between the market price and contract price.
The court held that the buyer's communication to the seller on
20 January asking for tender of documents was an
unequivocal representation for the purpose of waiver but it
was impossible to say that the seller had acted to his detriment
by relying on it.

Robert Goff J. stated that the seller had presented the
documents on the same day that the buyer made the request.
The seller had acted on this representation and conducted his
affairs by relying on it and although most of the elements of
waiver were present in the instruction on 20 January, these
elements were not operative.

Precise compliance is, therefore, required in mercantile contracts as
speedy declarations are regarded as being important, even though
no time limit may be given to send a notice of appropriation.

Progress test 8

1. What is a notice of appropriation and is it useful to have one?
(1)

2. What is its legal effect? Give examples. **(2)**

3. Can a notice of appropriation ever be revoked by a seller?
(3, 5)

4. What is the difference between appropriation and
unconditional appropriation? **(4)**

5. What is the effect of a notice of appropriation not being
received on time? **(5)**

6. What was the effect of the case of *The Post Chaser*? (1981) **(6)**

9
Free on board contracts

Introduction

1. Some initial considerations

The free on board contract was described by Devlin J. in the case of *Pyrene* v. *Scindia Navigation Co.* (1954) as 'a flexible instrument'. There is no rigid definition of what it is or should be, and neither is there such a thing as a standard free on board contract. The initials f.o.b. are usually used instead of the complete words and are normally followed by the name of the port of departure. The phrase is often used in relation to the delivery obligations of the parties.

Types of f.o.b. contracts and their obligations

2. The main types of f.o.b. contract

Devlin J. identified three types of f.o.b. contract in *Pyrene* v. *Scindia*, which are:

(a) classic;
(b) additional services; and
(c) strict.

Others have also been identified by other writers. Sassoon, for example, identifies three main types; Eric Davies in the *Business Law Review* 1956 recognises as many as nine variants; Professor Schmitthoff recognised two. The two main differing types are the *strict* and *additional services* (usually referred to as shipment to destination) f.o.b. contracts.

Although the f.o.b. contract has many variants, the basic elements of delivery, property and risk are common to them all.

3. The fundamental obligations of a strict f.o.b. contract

Here the obligations are weighted more to the buyer than to the seller.

(a) *The buyer's main obligations.* These are as follows:
  (*i*) To nominate an effective ship, which means to make all the necessary carriage arrangements for taking the goods from the contractual f.o.b. origin port within the shipment period. The shipment period runs for the benefit of the buyer.
  (*ii*) To give advance warning to the seller to be ready with the ship.
  (*iii*) To select the port of shipment. There may be a range of ports for him to choose from, when there will usually be an express clause in the contract to this effect. If not, then it is usually implied by the courts that written notice will be given.

(b) *The seller's obligations.* The seller's obligations are limited to the shipping of contract conforming goods, i.e. goods that correspond with the order made —

Pyrene v. *Scindia Navigation Co.* (1954): There was a contract for the sale of a fire tender under strict f.o.b. The buyer arranged the contract of carriage and the vessels arrived at their destination, but, during loading of the cargo, the fire tender was dropped and damaged. It had not yet crossed the ship's rail at the time of the accident and so the property had not yet passed to the buyer. The seller therefore sued the carrier in tort in order to recover the cost of repairing the damage.

The issue of the case was to determine the measure of the damages. The carrier tried relying on the limitation clause in the contract for a maximum of £200, as under the Hague Visby Rules, but the seller contended, first, that the fire tender had not crossed the ship's rail when it was being loaded, and so the accident was outside the period specified for application of the Hague Visby Rules.

Second, the Rules were not incorporated into the contract of carriage as a Bill of Lading had not been issued and, third, even if the Rules could be applied to this operation of loading, they had no application between the seller and carrier as the seller was not a party to the contract of carriage under the principal of privity of contract sales.

The court held that the carrier was to pay £200 to the seller. It also held that the rights and liabilities under the Hague Visby Rules did not attach to a period of time but to a *contract* and the whole act of loading was within the notion of a contract of carriage. Also, once a contract of carriage had been concluded and a Bill of Lading was being contemplated to be issued, then the contract of carriage was covered by a Bill of Lading for the purposes of the Hague Convention.

Finally, the inference should be drawn that it was the intention of all three parties that the seller should participate in the contract of carriage. The seller took such benefits as applied to their interests, subject to any qualifications that the contract imposed. Here the qualification was the limitation provision of £200.

Devlin J. stated that the seller is a party to the contract of carriage until he takes out a Bill of Lading in the buyer's name. Therefore, the rule in f.o.b. contracts is that *property passes in the goods when the goods are across the ship's rail.*

Devlin J. got around the privity problem in two ways. First, on the basis of agency, he said that the seller is a party to the contract to the extent of his involvement in it, i.e. by the loading process, thus there was a relationship between the seller and carrier.

Second, when the seller put the goods on the keystone for loading, he was making an offer to the carrier that the carrier accepted when he lifted the goods. There was therefore an implied contract between the seller and carrier based on the terms of the written contract.

4. Shipment to destination f.o.b.

This type of f.o.b. contract is frequently used when the buyer is small and has no presence in the f.o.b. origin port. The contract of sale will then provide that the seller does certain things on behalf of the buyer, unlike a strict f.o.b. contract where it will be the buyer's responsibility to carry out these activities.

The seller will arrange for:

(a) the carriage and insurance of the goods to their destination for the buyer;

(b) nominating an effective ship;

(c) choosing when during the shipment period he will be shipping the goods (if a range of ports is provided, then the seller must select and use such a port as he chooses from the range).

5. Comparison of f.o.b. and Cost Insurance Freight contracts

The above is similar to the seller's obligations in a Cost Insurance Freight contract but there are two major differences.

First, the nature of delivery. Under a Cost Insurance Freight contract, delivery is constructive, i.e. by documents, whereas under an f.o.b. contract, delivery is the physical presence of the goods on board ship, i.e. by virtue of the arrival of the goods themselves rather than of documents.

Second, the capacity in which the seller performs various tasks is different. Under a Cost Insurance Freight contract, everything the seller does for the buyer is done within a principal to principal relationship with clear responsibilities on both sides. For example, the seller cannot arrange the insurance because he will then be in breach of contract, unless a frustrating event occurs to mitigate the circumstances.

Under an f.o.b. contract, however, the seller only ships on board contract conforming goods acting for and on behalf of the buyer. Everything else the seller does will be done in his capacity as the buyer's agent. This difference in capacity results in two effects, as described below.

6. The effects of capacity
These are as follows:

(a) In acting as principal for the buyer, the seller under the f.o.b. destination contract is only held to a lower level of obligation, which means a principal to agent relationship rather than a principal to principal one as in a Cost Insurance Freight contract. The lower level of obligation is that the seller is an agent for the buyer, doing extra things for the buyer who is the principal. The only obligation is to exercise the best effort that the seller can for the principal.

(b) If there is some anticipated level of freight rate or insurance premium at the time of contracting that changes dramatically before the seller performs under the contract, then this increase will be passed on by the seller (agent) to the buyer (his principal). The risk in variation will, therefore, fall on the buyer, whereas in a Cost Insurance Freight contract it would fall on the seller.

It is therefore common for the seller to pass two invoices to the buyer — one relating to the goods, the other relating to charges for doing the extra things, plus commission for carrying out these activities as the buyer's agent.

7. Selection of the port of shipment
When a range of ports has been given in the contract, who selects the port of shipment from the range if this is not stipulated in the contract beforehand? —

> *Boyd* v. *Louis Louce* (1973): Kerr J. held that, in the absence of a named port of shipment, an express agreement, trade custom or any inference which can be drawn from surrounding circumstances, the choice of the loading port in a f.o.b. contract should be made by the buyer.
> The facts of the case were that there was a contract for the sale

of a quantity of Danish herring that provided for the delivery to be made in three instalments in successive months. A clause in the contract stipulated 'f.o.b. stowed good Danish port'. The buyer did not provide any shipping instructions or communication with the seller in any way and, towards the end of each month, the seller claimed that the buyer was in default. The court held that the naming of the port of shipment in an f.o.b. contract was the buyer's duty and right. Thus, where nothing has been agreed and there is no custom, the buyer must choose the port of shipment.

However, in practice, there is flexibility as to the port of shipment, which is intended for the seller's benefit as he may not know at the time of signing where exactly he will obtain the goods. He must, therefore, select carefully.

8.   The nomination of an effective vessel

Usually under an f.o.b. contract the buyer has the responsibility of nominating an effective vessel to be used for the voyage, should one not be stipulated in the contract of sale.

The buyer then has to inform the seller of the name of the ship on which the goods are to be carried, along with its readiness to load. This must all be communicated to the seller within a reasonable time to allow the seller to get the goods ready.

Bunge v. *Tradax*: The buyer's notification was ineffective because it reached the seller too late, which entitled the seller to reject and sue for non-acceptance under the contract.

This duty of the f.o.b. buyer was reinforced by Lord Hewart CJ in *J. and J. Cunningham Ltd* v. *Robert A. Monroe Ltd* (1922):

... the usual practice under such a contract is for the buyer to nominate a vessel and to send notice of her arrival to the vendor, in order that the vendor may be in a position to fulfil his part of the contract.

It follows, therefore, that under a f.o.b. contract, the *time* within which a vessel must be nominated is vitally important to the success of the contract. Should this not be followed then it will amount to a breach of a condition of the contract. The buyer is entitled, therefore, to repudiate the contract on such grounds — *see The Osterbeck* (1972).

The ship nominated must be suitable for its task, otherwise it will amount to a breach of contract in the seller's favour — *see Compagnie* v. *Seymour Plant Sales & Hire Ltd* (1981).

9.   The nomination of a substitute vessel

Usually, as we have seen, the buyer must nominate an effective vessel, but if the first nomination fails and the original vessel becomes unavailable for some reason, then a substitute vessel may still be nominated by the buyer, provided loading can be completed within the contract period —

> *Agricultores* v. *Ampo SA* (1965): Here a seller sold a quantity of maize f.o.b. Rosario, shipment to be from 20–29 September 1960. The buyer nominated a vessel but she was delayed by rain and it became apparent that she could not be loaded until 30 September, the day after the contract would expire. At 4 p.m. on 29 September, the seller informed the buyer that they intended to cancel the contract because the vessel nominated by them had not arrived. However, at 4.30 p.m. the buyer managed to engage another vessel, which was at Rosario and was capable of carrying the goods.
>
> The seller, however, refused to co-operate and undertake the arrangements that were required in order to enable the second vessel to load within the contract time.
>
> It was held by the court that the seller's behaviour evinced an intention not to perform their contract and that the buyer was entitled to treat the failure as an anticipatory breach and a repudiation of the contract. The allegation that the buyer could not withdraw the vessel originally nominated and nominate a substitute vessel to perform as per the contract therefore failed. There is no limit to the number of successive vessels that can be nominated *as long as loading takes place within the contract period*.
>
> Widgery J. in this case stated that although the buyer had nominated the first vessel, this had not inhibited him from changing his mind and substituting another vessel, provided the new vessel was capable of accepting the cargo within the time for shipment stipulated in the contract.

Should another nomination *not* fall within the contract time, however, the buyer will be in default. The seller would then be entitled to claim damages for the buyer's delay. This rule applies even if failure to nominate a vessel on time is due to unforeseen circumstances —

> *Colley* v. *Overseas Exporters* (1921): The buyer prevented the property passing to him by failing to nominate the ship on which the goods were to be carried. In the case, the right to

payment for goods sold would arise upon their being loaded
onto a ship nominated by the buyer, but the buyer refused to
name a ship. The seller was therefore unable to recover the
price of the goods. (The case also serves to illustrate that if no
time limit has been stipulated within the contract as to when
nomination is to take place, reasonable time will apply.)

10. Notice of arrival

There is usually a requirement that the buyer gives the seller
notice of when the nominated vessel is to arrive, otherwise the seller
will not know when the buyer may call for the shipment during the
shipment period. Failure to give such notice will be a major breach
of the contract as such a term is a condition of the contract and so the
buyer will be entitled to rescind it.

This was decided by the House of Lords in the case of *Bunge* v.
Tradax (1981).

> *Bunge* v. *Tradax* (1981): The buyer agreed to buy from the
> seller a quantity of US soya bean meal 'f.o.b. one US Gulf port
> at SS option stoned and trimmed'. The buyers were to give the
> seller 15 days' notice of the vessel's nomination and readiness
> to receive goods. However, this was given late, on 17 instead
> of 14 June. The issue to be decided was whether this notice of
> arrival clause for 15 days was a condition or an innominate
> term. The buyer contended that it was an innominate term. It
> was held to be a condition of the contract that was a necessary
> part of the buyer's obligations.
> Lord Wilberforce said that it is essential that both buyers and
> sellers know precisely what their obligations are, most
> especially because the ability of the seller to fulfil his
> obligations may well be totally dependent on punctual
> performance by the buyer. A time clause can only be breached
> by being late. Certainty is, therefore, the most indispensable
> quality of mercantile contracts.

Halsbury's Laws of England (4th Edition, Volume 9) states that:

(a) the court will require precise compliance with stipulations as to
time wherever the circumstances of the case indicate that this will
fulfil the intention of the parties; and
(b) time will be considered to be of the essence in mercantile
contracts.

In *Bunge* v. *Tradax* (1981), the time limit was specific, but this is not always the case — *see Gill & Duffus* v. *Societé* (1986). In this case there was no fixed time limit as to when the notice of arrival of the vessel was to be given. It was held that the buyer must give enough time for arrival.

If enough time is not given to the seller on the vessel's arrival, then the seller can either repudiate the contract or start to load the cargo on board the late vessel.

If the seller decided to do this then the seller's duty is to load as much as can be loaded within the delivery period specified in the contract, but his obligation ceases at the end of that period, i.e. he is under no obligation to continue loading after that period expires — *see Bunge* v. *Tradax* (1975). Donaldson J. in the case stated that, 'Under an f.o.b. contract, the obligation to delivery and the obligation to accept delivery are mutual and both are confined to the shipment period'.

11. Additional charges

If nomination of the vessel is not made in time but the seller nevertheless loads the cargo beyond the shipment period, then he should be compensated for additional carrying charges that may occur as a result from the buyer —

Miserocchi v. *AFA* (1982): Three contracts were concluded on a GAFTA form 64 in which the parties sold quantities of Argentinian maize. All three contracts were f.o.b. Rosario or Buenos Aires June 1978.

In March there was heavy rainfall that made the roads to the ports impassable. There was therefore a delay in delivery of the vessels. Because the ships chartered by the buyer were delayed in entering the ports, the seller claimed the resulting extra carriage charges for the maize. The buyer paid the charges on one contract but refused to pay them on the other two. It was held that the buyer had to pay all the carrying charges.

The view of Staughton J. was that this was a strict f.o.b. contract and so the basic obligation to nominate a vessel falls on the buyer and so any extra costs resulting from failure to do so were to be borne by the buyer.

It is the buyer's obligation to provide a ship at the place of shipment on the day when shipment is to take place. The seller must then bring his goods to the ship's rail for loading. The precise time of arrival is the province of the buyer because it is his duty to provide a ship.

A buyer must bear the losses caused by any congestion or delay. If the buyer commits himself, he will be bound to perform as per the contract no matter what, unless it can be shown that there is a frustrating event or that the buyer is protected by a clause in the contract.

Here in the *Miserocchi* v. *AFA* (1982) case, the buyer claimed that there was an implied term in such contracts that there would be an available berth, but this was rejected as being mere business efficacy. It was not necessary to imply a term because it was a strict f.o.b. contract with the obligation to nominate falling on the buyer. Any extra cost arising from failure to do this was therefore the buyer's.

It is the buyer who is also responsible for any additional expenses incurred as a result of a *substitute* vessel being nominated. He can also be held liable for failure to nominate the substitute vessel within the time stipulated in the contract.

However, if the buyer can show that he could not have nominated a substitute vessel to fall within the stipulated contract period, then he would not be held personally liable. Alternatively, this will also apply if the time period can be extended by implied terms or a custom of the trade.

Progress test 9

1. What is an f.o.b. contract?   **(1, 2)**

2. How does it differ to a Cost Insurance Freight contract? **(2, 3)**

3. What is the difference between a strict f.o.b. contract and a shipment to destination f.o.b. contract?   **(1, 4, 5)**

4. Does the buyer have to specify the port of shipment? If so, why?   **(7)**

5. Who has to nominate an effective substitute vessel?   **(8, 9)**

6. What is the effect if the seller does not comply with the buyer's instructions?   **(10, 11)**

10
Licences

Export licences

1. Fundamental issues

There are three fundamental issues to be aware of when considering export licences. These are:

(a) whose obligation it is to get the licence when one is necessary;
(b) the nature and extent of the obligation, i.e. whether it is an absolute one or one of best effort or due diligence;
(c) whether due diligence has been exercised for the purposes of getting the licence.

2. Whose obligation is it to organise licences?

In Cost Insurance Freight and Arrival contracts, it is the seller's obligation, but in f.o.b. contracts, it can be either the buyer's or the seller's. In these cases the contract will usually specify who is to organise it. If it does not, then the buyer will be obliged to obtain it —

> *Brandt* v. *Morris* (1917): There was a domestic f.o.b. contract as both buyer and seller were in the UK. The buyer contracted to sell to overseas sub-buyers 60 tons of aniline oil f.o.b. Manchester, UK. After the contract was signed, an order was issued prohibiting the export of this product without a licence. Some goods were exported before the ban but not all. The buyer left it to the seller to get the licence and later sued for non-delivery.
> It was held that the obligation of applying for and obtaining the necessary licence lay upon the buyer and not the seller so the action failed.
> Scrutton L.J. stated in his judgment that the buyer had to provide 'an effective ship', i.e. a ship that can legally carry the goods.

Viscount Reading C.J. went on to further explain the buyer's duty '. . . to find the ship, the facts which are necessary to state when a licence is applied for were known to the buyer. All that the sellers know in such a case is that they have sold the goods to the buyers.

A gap of a number of years followed this ruling, but it was eventually clarified by *Pound* v. *Hardy* (1956). Here the House of Lords said that the *Brandt* v. *Morris* (1917) case could not lay down a fixed rule because it was decided on its own facts —

> *Pound* v. *Hardy* (1956): A contract was entered into between a UK seller and a US buyer to buy Portuguese turpentine from the UK seller free along side (f.a.s.) Lisbon. The UK seller was getting the turpentine from his Portuguese supplier. Under Portuguese regulations only an export licence was needed, which could only be obtained by a supplier registered with the Portuguese authorities. The contract was silent as to whose obligation it was to obtain the export licence. Because the destination was the then Iron Curtain country Germany, the seller failed to obtain the export licence. The buyer was unwilling to nominate a substitute destination so the contract could not be performed. The seller sued for damages of breach of contract.
>
> It was held by the House of Lords that the duty to secure the necessary export licence lay with the seller, not the buyer, as only the seller knew the identity of the Portuguese suppliers who could apply.

Thus, although the *Pound* v. *Hardy* (1956) case did not follow the ruling of the *Brandt* v. *Morris* (1917) case, it avoided laying down any rule of general application. It does, however, show that the respective obligations of the parties in a f.o.b. contract will depend on the surrounding circumstances of the contract. Usually, though, it is the seller who has to obtain the export licence.

There is a duty to co-operate once the obligation duty has been obtained —

> *Kyprianou* v. *Cyprus Textiles* (1958): In order to obtain the export licence, the applicant had to say that the goods were not going to Israel. The seller needed the buyer to certify this but the buyer refused to give such a guarantee.
>
> It was held that the seller was not in breach of the contract as the buyer had not co-operated with him to get the export

licence. Before a seller can be made liable for breach of an obligation to obtain an export licence, the buyer must have furnished him with all the details that may be necessary for such a purpose.

3. Types of obligation

Is there a *best effort* or *due diligence obligation* or is there an *absolute obligation*? If there is an absolute obligation that is not fulfilled, then the contract will have been breached. However, if there is a best effort obligation that is not fulfilled, the contract will not have been broken, so there will have been no breach.

4. Absolute obligation

This raises the question of the construction of the contract and the circumstances of the case —

Atisa v. *Aztec* (1983): A clause in the contract specified that 'the seller shall be responsible for obtaining any necessary export licences. Failure to obtain such licences shall not be sufficient grounds for a claim of *force majeure* if the regulations in force at the time the contract is made call for such licences to be obtained'.

It was held that the seller was under an *absolute obligation* to get the export licence; failure led to a breach of the contract.

If one knows, therefore, about the licensing restrictions when a contract is made, then there is an absolute obligation, but if, for example, there is an unexpected coup, just the best effort obligation is required as the circumstances are unpredictable —

Portabmull Ramashwar v. *Sethia* (1951): There was a contract for the sale of jute to be shipped f.o.b. India. There was a quota system in operation and the seller could not get an export licence for the jute as he had exceeded his quota for export in the previous year and so could not ship the goods.

The court held that the seller was in breach for failing to ship the goods as he *knew* of the Indian government restrictions. The seller's obligation to obtain the export licence was therefore an absolute one.

Peter Cassidy Seed Co. v. *Osuustukkuk-Auppa I.L.* (1957): Here, too, there was an absolute obligation because of the wording of a clause in the contract. The facts were that there was a contract to purchase a quantity of ants' eggs f.o.b. Helsinki. A clause in the contract read, 'Delivery: prompt as soon as export licence is granted'. The seller admitted that it was his duty to obtain the necessary export licence but that he was unable to secure it as the company was not a member of the Ants' Egg Association.

Devlin J. held that the seller was liable for damages suffered by the buyer because the particular language of the contract imposed an absolute obligation on the seller.

5.   Best effort obligation

If the contract fails to stipulate a term relating to export prohibition, then it will be a best effort obligation only. Once there is an absolute obligation, the seller will *always* have to obtain the export licence *unless* he is protected by a clause in the contract —

Anglo-Russian Trader & John Batt (1971): There was no clause in the contract as to the nature of the seller's obligation. It was held that the obligation was only to do one's best.

Colinale Import Export v. *Loumides* (1978): At first instance, the court reviewed the pre-1978 cases and stated that *only if there is a clause in the contract dealing with the nature of the obligation will the courts construe it to be an absolute obligation.* If there is no expressed term as to the nature of the obligation, it will be one of best effort.

Pagnan v. *Tradax* (1987): There was a contract for the sale of tapioca f.o.b. Thailand to Italy. A quota system was in operation, the seller had exceeded their quota and so could not ship the goods. There were two clauses in the contract. The first clause stated, 'Seller to provide export certificate enabling the buyer to obtain the export licence into the EEC'.
The second stated, 'In case of prohibition on export, blockade . . . etc., restricting export, any such restriction shall be deemed to apply to the contract and any unfulfilled portion therefore shall be cancelled'.
It was held by the courts that the first clause created an absolute obligation on the part of the seller as it was an additional special clause. Regarding the second clause, however, there was no absolute obligation on the part of the seller, and so he was not in breach as he could rely on the prohibition clause, which was a standard clause. The second clause therefore prevailed. The first could not as there was no consistency between the two clauses in the same contract.

6. How can you tell if best effort has been exercised?

The test for exertion of best effort is whether there has been a continuity of effort made by the party on whom the obligation rests. This continuity is applied over the shipment period. An exception does apply if it becomes futile to make any further effort to secure the licence as the continuity will be interrupted and no further effort therefore needs to be made —

> *Malik* v. *Central European Trading Agency* (1974): There was a contract of sale for 500 tons of Sudanese sesame seeds Cost Insurance Freight Ancora and the shipment period was between January and February, subject to an export licence being obtained. In the third week of February, the seller realised that an export licence was required and so applied for it but it was refused so no goods were shipped. The buyer sued for non-delivery.
> It was held that the seller was in breach of contract because he had not exerted his best effort in obtaining the export licence. He should have started to apply for the licence much earlier than he did. There was no evidence to indicate that if the seller had applied earlier that the licence would have been refused then as well.

A similar case is *Compagnie Continentale* v. *Ispahani* (1962), which illustrates that a seller must show that all possible steps were taken to obtain a licence or that it was pointless so to do —

> *Provimi Hellas* v. *Warinco* (1978): There was a contract for the sale of soya beans '. . . f.o.b. Perasus, shipment before 15 June'. The seller had been granted an export licence on 25 May but on 7 June it was suspended.
> From 8–12 June, various vigorous efforts were made by both the buyer and the seller (although it was only the seller's duty, co-operation was needed to get the export licence reinstated — they went as far as to interview the general economic adviser and the Greek prime minister. No further efforts were made after 12 June. The buyer sued, claiming damages for non-delivery.
> It was held that, as there was no written prospect of securing an export licence within the shipment period, further applications would have been futile so no further efforts were required and the seller was discharged from his obligations as he was not required to waste effort on a futile task.

Import licences

7. Where the obligations lie

The general position is that there is no obligation on either party to get an import licence, rather it is something that the buyer must do in his own interest —

Congimex v. *Tradax* (1983): There was no implied term in the contract that buyers were under an absolute duty to obtain an import licence.

Colinale Import Export v. *Loumides* (1978): Clause 30 in the contract was only designed to establish whose duty it was to obtain the import licence, but it left open the *nature* of this duty. The reason for this was that the word 'responsibility' in clause 30 of the contract was not strong enough to establish an absolute obligation.

Progress test 10

1. Who has the duty of obtaining the export licence under an f.o.b. contract? **(1, 2)**

2. What effort is needed to obtain an export licence? **(3, 4, 5)**

3. What is the effect of 'best effort' not being exercised? Give an example. **(6)**

4. Who has the duty of obtaining the import licence under an f.o.b. contract? **(7)**

11
Frustration

Introduction

1. The effect of frustration

Under English Law, obligations are absolute unless expressly qualified in the contract. However, this rule has been mitigated by the doctrine of frustration.

What it is and how it is pleaded

2. What is frustration?

Frustration occurs when the parties are unable to perform their obligation as intended when they entered the contract due to some unforeseen event.

3. Ways in which frustration can occur

There are three main ways in which a contract can be frustrated. There are:

(a) *Illegality*. Where performance of the contract has become illegal after its conclusion, e.g. should there be an outbreak of war between the buyer and seller countries or the imposition of an absolute prohibition or any licensing restrictions.

(b) *Destruction of subject matter*. Where performance of the contract has become objectively impossible due to the subject matter being destroyed — *see BP Exploration* v. *Hunt No.2* (1979). In the case the withdrawal of concessions destroyed the subject matter of the contract, resulting in the contract being mitigated by frustration.

(c) *Fundamental change in circumstances*. Where there has been a fundamental change in circumstances so that performance would hold the parties to something different to what was originally agreed and anticipated at the time of contracting, then frustration occurs. This is a difficult category to plead. It is best illustrated by the various coronation and funeral cases where windows have been hired to view a procession but the route is then diverted, etc.

Frustration is not easy to invoke —

> *Lewis Emanuel* v. *Sammut* (1959): Here the contract was for the sale of potatoes to be shipped from Malta to London. The contract was entered into on 14 April, shipment was to be made by 24 April, which was a very short shipping period. During that period only one ship called to London via Malta and all the space on it was fully booked. The seller could not therefore ship the goods within the shipping period. The buyer sued for non-delivery. The seller pleaded frustration on the grounds that the contract had become impossible to perform.
>
> It was held by Pearson J. that it was not a frustrating event as there was nothing unusual, extraordinary or exceptional in the circumstances and it has to be something *not normally anticipated* for frustration to occur. It was advised that it was best to insert a clause in the contract saying 'subject to shipment' or 'subject to a licence being obtained'.

4. Self-induced frustration

If a party brings about the happening of the frustrating event, then the benefit of the doctrine cannot be claimed —

> *Czarnikow* v. *Rolimpex* (1978): There was a *force majeure* clause contract for 2000 tons of sugar sold to Czarnikow by Rolimpex. The *force majeure* clause stated that 'if delivery is prevented by government intervention beyond the seller's control', then the contract will be void without penalty.
>
> In 1974 there were heavy rains and floods in Poland so the sugar beet crop was poor. Later on in the year, a general export prohibition was imposed on any sugar product. The seller relied on the *force majeure* clause and notified the buyer that the contract could not be performed, but the buyer sued for non-delivery.
>
> It was held that the buyer's argument that it was self-induced frustration was not acceptable. However, the court went no further than to examine the independent legal personality of Rolimpex and said that, despite the ties between the departments of state and the state trading agencies, it was a separate legal entity.

The fact that performance would be more costly and that the seller would have to acquire goods at a price exceeding the one he agreed to sell them for, is not sufficient to frustrate the contract —

Brauer & Co. v. *James Clark Ltd* (1952): The Brazilian government fixed a minimum price limit for certain commodities that resulted in an increase in the price of the contract goods so that export licences could not be procured if the transactions were to be based on the price prevailing at the date of the agreement. It was held that, although the seller had to pay more to get the licence, the contract was not frustrated as the circumstances must be unforeseeable. However, Lord Denning in the case stated that the cost could be so great as to result in a different situation altogether. For example, if one had to pay 100 times more, then that would amount to frustration.

Exportelisa v. *Rocco Guiseppe* (1978): There was a contract for 5000 tons of wheat at $230 per ton to be sent f.o.b. Necochea. The seller invoked an exemption clause to relieve him of liability if performance was to become impossible by virtue of an export ban.
It was held that the seller was not excused from performance as they could still have bought the goods — albeit at a higher price — from another seller in Argentina.

Therefore, where the effect of the government monopoly is merely to increase the price of the goods so that the seller can only fulfil his obligation at a loss, the seller *cannot* rely on an exemption clause to relieve him from liability for non-performance because of an impossibility created by an export ban.

5.   State immunity
This same approach has been taken on the issue of state immunity —

Trendtex Trading Corp. v. *Central Bank of Nigeria* (1977): In this case, the Central Bank of Nigeria issued letters of credit and Trendtex was a beneficiary of one of these letters, which was to finance military barracks, etc. There was a change in government and the Bank was instructed not to honour certain letters of credit.
Trentex and others sought to sue the Bank in the English

courts. The Bank contended that it was entitled to remain outside the UK jurisdiction due to state immunity.

The issue in the case was whether the Bank could be entitled to claim such state immunity even though it was a commercial transaction. It was later held that the Bank was a separate legal entity, not an organisation of the State of Nigeria, and, therefore, it could not rely on the doctrine of state immunity. As a result, Trendtex *et al.* were able to sue the Bank through the English courts. The court took the same approach as in *Czarnikow* v. *Rolimpex* (1978) (*ante*).

Progress test 11

1. What is frustration?   **(1)**

2. What effect does it have upon a contract?   **(1, 2)**

3. What are the ways in which a frustrating event can occur?   **(3)**

4. What is self-induced frustration; how does it affect the contract?   **(4)**

12
Force majeure clauses

Introduction

1. What are the *force majeure* clauses?

Force majeure clauses are common in contracts of sale and have the effect of specifying which events will amount to frustration and the consequences of such events occurring. The main types of events are usually bad weather, embargos or strikes. In such circumstances, the parties will be discharged from performance of the contract. The Grain and Feed Trade Association (GAFTA) form 100 embraces such *force majeure* clauses, which appear in clauses 21 and 22 of the contract.

Clauses 21 and 22 of form 100

2. Clause 21

Clause 21 deals with events that prohibit export. It relates to governmental acts that give rise to a prohibition of export.

3. Clause 22

Clause 22 deals with events that cause a delay in shipment. However, it does not lead to cancellation of the contract, as would be the case with clause 21. Instead, it introduces an element of contractual adjustment if one of the events arise that will lead to delay.

Clause 22 involves some precise times as to when notices are to be given. If the terms of the clause are adhered to, then they can delay shipment up to one month. There can be an additional month of postponement of the seller's performance, but if shipment does not take place after the end of the month's postponement, then the contract will be void. Clause 22 is therefore flexible as to the seller's obligation but is more strict as to time as the time is a maximum of two months before the contract becomes void.

Clause 22 of form 100 was at issue in the following case —

Toepfer v. *Cremer* (1975): In the case, flooding caused havoc to the soya bean crop so the government imposed restrictions on the exporter of the soya beans. In essence, an embargo was imposed suddenly and took immediate effect. However, there was a loophole in the embargo, permitting an exception for goods already on lighters destined for an exporting vessel or for which loading on board an exporting vessel had actually commenced as of 5 p.m. on 24 June. On 2 July, the US government said it would give a licence allowing 40 per cent of the shipment to take place. The court held that clause 22 could be relied on as the notice was sufficient. However, the goods were still not shipped during the extension period and therefore they were in default. The main issue in the case was as to the damages as soya bean prices had gone up during this period.

This governmental intervention gave rise to hundreds of disputes. The first case to come to court as a result was in 1976 — *Tradax* v. *André*. Lord Denning was quoted as saying '. . . over 500 arbitrations are awaiting the result of this case'.

Lord Roskill in 1979 also stated that '. . . soya bean cases have harrassed the Court of Appeal and so the flow goes on'. Most of the disputes arose because the seller in each case had not shipped the goods required by 27 June when the government restriction came into operation.

4. What the seller must prove to use clause 21

The seller must show that he has no goods on a lighter or in the course of loading that would be outside the scope of the embargo. He must also show that he does not come within any of the loopholes in the prohibition. To do this, the seller must go back through the string to the original shipper. Usually this cannot be done, so sellers cannot often succeed in using clause 21.

Brown L.J. in the *Tradax* v. *André* (1976) case noted that if prohibition has exceptions or relaxations, then the seller must prove that he does not fall within them.

The question was taken up in *Bremer* v. *Vanden* (1978) when the case reached the House of Lords. In the House of Lords a distinction was drawn between an *absolute* and a *partial* prohibition. If there is an absolute prohibition, then the seller does not have to prove that he had the goods ready to ship within the contract period and a ship to carry them. The House of Lords also concluded that a seller has no obligation to buy goods afloat in order to implement the contract —

> *Warinco* v. *Mauther* (1978): There was a contract for the sale of goods Cost Insurance Freight Rotterdam. Shipment was to be from a Mediterranean port. The Cost Insurance Freight seller arranged to fulfil the contract by buying goods from a supplier f.o.b. Peraus, but the Greek government's intervention prevented him from shipping the goods, so he tried to rely on clause 22 of form 100.
> In the first instance this argument succeeded, and he did not have to perform in alternative ways if the main way failed, which is similar to Lord Denning's pronouncement in *Tradax* v. *André* (1976), but the Court of Appeal reversed the decision and said that although the way he intended was impossible, he could ship another way. The seller was therefore in breach of contract and, as a result, could not rely on clause 21.

5. Limited supplies

What happens if a seller has a number of contracts but has a limited supply of goods and therefore cannot fulfil all the contracts? —

> *Hong Guan* v. *Jamabhoy* (1960): A Privy Council case, there was a contract for the sale of Zanzibar cloves. The seller could not obtain sufficient supplies to fulfil his contracts. Clause 21 in the contract stipulated, 'Subject to shipment and *force majeure*'. The seller chose to allocate the limited supply of the goods that he had to other contracts. The buyer was told that his contract was cancelled and, as a result, he claimed for non-delivery.
> It was held that the seller was in breach of contract as the words 'Subject to shipment' meant that the contract was conditional on being able to obtain shipment. They would have performed the contract but chose not to do so. The seller was therefore in breach as the situation was similar to self-induced frustration.
> However, Dicta in the case stressed that where there is partial shortage, a buyer can sue for non-delivery if the choice was left to the seller as to which contracts were to be performed.

In later cases the courts have adopted a more helpful approach by saying that if there is a limited supply, then as long as there has been reasonable allocation of the goods it will be acceptable — *see Intertradax* v. *Lasieur-Tourteaux* 1978).

> *Pancommerce* v. *Veecheema* (1982): The seller contracted with X to sell 1500 tons of sugarbeet. The seller stated that if they got any further supplies that year, X would be given first refusal on a further 1500 tons. The seller also contracted to sell 1500 tons to Y. However, the seller could only get a export licence to ship 3000 tons due to an embargo imposed by the Spanish Ministry of Commerce. As a result, he gave the first 1500 to X and he split the second 1500 between X and Y.
> It was held by the Court of Appeal that he was wrong to do so as there was no *contractual* obligation to give first refusal to X. He should have given 1500 to X *and* 1500 to Y. The seller was therefore in breach of contract for failing to ship the correct amount to Y. This kind of division of the available supply between a contractual claimant and someone less puts the seller in breach to the contractual claimant for the entire amount of the available undershipment.

6. Point of assessing damages

Section 51 of the Sale of Goods Act 1979 states that, prima facie, the measure of damages is the difference between the contract price and the market price at the date of the breach. This rule can be displaced by a contractual provision. For example, GAFTA form 100, clause 26 imposes an obligation on the buyer to go out into the market to buy alternative goods and then to claim the difference between the contracted price and the price he paid for them. This clause 26 displaces s. 51 of the Sale of Goods Act 1979.

Progress test 12

1. What is a *force majeure* clause? **(1)**

2. What effect will such a clause have upon a contract? **(1)**

3. What are the effects of clauses 21 and 22 of GAFTA form 100? **(2, 3)**

4. What is the position where the seller cannot fulfil contracts due to limited supplies? **(5)**

5. How are damages assessed according to s. 51 of the Sale of Goods Act 1979? **(6)**

13

The passing of property

Introduction

1. Why do we need to know that property has passed?
There are several reasons why it is necessary to know whether property has passed.

(a) *To determine whether risk has passed.* Section 20 of the Sale of Goods Act 1979 states that risk passes when property passes. This is more relevant to domestic transactions but in international transactions this view has been displaced and risk passes on shipment, e.g. in Cost Insurance Freight contracts (*ante*).
In strict f.o.b. contracts, risk *and* property pass together, whereas under a shipment to destination-type f.o.b. contract the situation is similar to that for Cost Insurance Freight.

(b) *The ability to sue for the price.* Property must have passed to be able to sue for the price under s. 1 of the Bills of Lading Act 1855.

(c) *In order to prove the tort of negligence.* To do this, one must have possession of the goods — *see The Aliakmon* (1982).

(d) *An action for the price of the goods will depend on whether property has passed in line with s. 49 of the Sale of Goods Act 1979.* It is better to sue for the price of the goods rather than damages because then the seller does not have to deal with the goods any further, while for damages, the seller will have to have dealt with the goods.

(e) *If the buyer or seller become insolvent.* Who owns the goods will depend on the passing of property. For example, if the seller is bankrupt, the buyer can say property has passed to him and so the goods can be claimed by him and vice versa.

Example
_____

The seller is a company and property has passed, therefore the buyer can have a good claim against the liquidator *even though* the goods are still in the seller's possession because the *property has passed to the buyer*. Otherwise the buyer would be an unsecured creditor and get nothing.

_____

(f) *If someone has obtained property in the goods then that person can pass the property on to give someone else a good title.* This is an exception to the *nemo dat.* rule (4:9).

The major sections on the passing of property are ss. 16–19 of the Sale of Goods Act 1979, which apply both to Cost Insurance Freight and f.o.b. contracts.

The time at which ownership passes to the buyer will depend on whether the goods are *specific* or *unascertained*.

The Sale of Goods Act 1979

2.   Section 16 and how it acts as a pre-condition

This section must be satisfied before any other section can be relevant or mean anything. Section 16 is, therefore, a precondition to be satisfied for the passing of property. Section 16 relates to *unascertained* goods.

Section 16, in essence, states that where there is a contract for unascertained goods, that no property in the goods will pass to the buyer until those goods are ascertained, i.e. set aside, identified, labelled, etc. as per the contract. Sometimes a notice of appropriation is enough to ascertain the goods, e.g. 1000 tons of the freight mentioned in the contract being carried on board a ship that is only carrying that 1000 tons.

3.   Mixed goods

If these same goods are mixed, for example 5000 tons are identical but others not, then the goods cannot be ascertained until they arrive and have been apportioned between the various buyers. Here a notice of appropriation could not serve to ascertain the goods within the meaning of s. 16 of the Sale of Goods Act 1979.

4.   Romalpa clauses

While goods remain in an unascertained state they cannot be identified as belonging to the buyer. However, even though goods have been ascertained they may still not belong to the buyer as there may be a Romalpa clause written into the contract according to s. 19 of the Sale of Goods Act 1979 —

> *Laurie & Harewood* v. *John Durdin & Sons* (1926): Here
> property was held not to have passed in 200 quarters of maize
> that were part of an individual larger bulk stored in a

warehouse. Property cannot therefore pass in an unidentified part of a larger shipment.

5. Ascertainment by exhaustion

Once unascertained goods have become ascertained the property or ownership will pass to the buyer. However, unascertained goods can also become ascertained by ascertainment by exhaustion — *see The Elafi* (1981).

> *Eastpoint Navigation Co.* (1982): Buyers in Hamburg, Rotterdam and Sweden each contracted to buy some of the copra that was loaded as a bulk shipment of 22 840 tons in the Philippines. The plaintiff Swedish buyers contracted at first for 6000 tons and later for a further 840 tons. A total of 16 000 tons was unloaded in Rotterdam and Hamburg, but some 1000 tons of the remaining shipment was then damaged because of the unseaworthiness of the ship.
>
> The question arose as to whether the plaintiff could sue on the ground that their goods were damaged. The court used the principle of ascertainment by exhaustion, as the remaining 6840 tons were all destined for the plaintiffs.

6. Section 17

Section 17 relates to specific goods. It is the key section to the passing of property.

Section 17(1) establishes the principle that property passes when the parties intend it to pass. Section 17(2) has a sweeping provision as to where one looks for evidence to determine the intention of the parties.

7. Intention

To find the intention, the terms of the contract, conduct of the parties, and circumstances of the case need to be looked at. However, it must be noted with regard to the terms of the contract that many standard form contracts include a retention of title clause, the effect being that property does not pass to the buyer until the price has been paid.

An example of s. 17 in operation can be found in the following case:

> *Anchor Line, Re* (1937): The buyer agreed to buy a dockside crane for a deferred purchase price of £40 000. The arrangement meant that he also paid a sum annually to the

seller by way of depreciation and interest, such sums then being deducted from the total purchase price. However, the buyer went into liquidation and the seller claimed the property in the goods.

The Court of Appeal found an intention that the property should remain with the seller until the full purchase price had been paid. Under the contract, the seller was receiving payment for the depreciation and this could only be the concern of the owner of the goods.

Despite the wideness of s. 17, it can sometimes still prove difficult to find the intention of the parties. When this situation arises, one has to refer to s. 18 of the Sale of Goods Act 1979.

8. Section 18

Section 18 provides 5 guidelines to determine the intention of the parties. These are merely meant to assist users rather than be thought of as legal rules. They are all mutually exclusive:

(a) rule 1 relates to specific goods in a deliverable state;
(b) rule 2 relates to specific goods not in a deliverable state;
(c) rule 3 relates to goods delivered to the buyer;
(d) rule 4 relates to goods on approval or on a sale or return basis or other similar terms;
(e) rule 5 relates to unascertained or future goods.

One usually starts out with unascertained goods, i.e. goods not identified at the time of contracting, and so rule 5 is often the most relevant as it relates to contracts for the sale of unascertained or future goods.

Each of the rules is now discussed in further detail.

9. Rule 1

This rule states:

Where there is an unconditional contract for sale of specific goods in a deliverable state, the property in the goods passes to the buyer when the contract is made and it is immaterial whether the time of payment or time of delivery, or both, be postponed.

Under this rule, the ownership of goods may be transferred to the buyer even though they are still in the seller's possession.

10. The meaning of 'unconditional'

An unconditional contract is one where conditions need to be fulfilled by the buyer before the title or ownership can be ascribed to him. If payment of the price first is required, for example, then it will be a conditional contract.

11. Specific Goods

Rule 1 only covers specific goods as defined in s. 61 —

Kursell v. *Timber Operators* (1927): Here the plaintiffs sold to the defendants those trees growing on an estate that conformed to certain minimum measurement requirements. The buyer was to cut and remove such trees as they attained the prescribed measurements, but in any case within 15 years. The forest was subsequently expropriated.
It was held by the Court of Appeal that the property (ownership) in the trees had not passed to the defendants because the goods were not sufficiently identified by the contract to enable them to be ascertained when the contract of sale was made.

12. Deliverable state

Rule 1 also requires that the goods be in a 'deliverable state'. As s. 61(5) states it, goods are in a deliverable state when they are in such a condition that the buyer would be bound to take delivery of them in performance of the contract. A buyer has the right to reject goods that do not satisfy the terms of the contract when they are tendered for delivery — see *Underwood* v. *Burgh Castle Brick & Cement Syndicate* (1922).

The following case illustrates the operation and importance of Rule 1 in general.

Dannant v. *Skinner & Collom* (1948): The buyer attended a motor auction. His bid was accepted by the auctioneer and the hammer fell, so there was then a contract between the buyer and seller. At the end of the auction, the buyer offered the seller a cheque for the car but the seller was reluctant to accept this. He agreed that the buyer should be in possession of the car but that the property should not pass until the cheque was cleared. The cheque was dishonoured, but the buyer re-sold the car to another buyer. The seller therefore sued the latest buyer for the car.
It was held that when the hammer fell the property had passed

under rule 1. The effect of the subsequent transaction was merely that the buyer had persuaded the seller to give up his lien on the goods. Property had passed to the rogue on the making of the contract and he passed good title to the defendant when he re-sold the vehicle. The plaintiff's case therefore failed.

13. Exclusion of rule 1

It is possible for the parties to exclude the operation of rule 1 by stipulating in the contract when ownership in the goods is to pass. An example of such phrasing could be, ownership ' . . . will pass even though the goods are not yet in a deliverable state as they are still under construction'.

Rule 1 specifies that goods must be in a deliverable state, so merely being transportable does not make them deliverable — it will depend on the terms of the contract. Where specific goods are not in a deliverable state, s. 18 rule 2 will apply.

14. Rule 2

This rule states that:

Where there is a contract for the sale of specific goods and the seller is bound to do something to the goods for the purpose of putting them into a deliverable state, the property does not pass until the thing is done and the buyer has notice that it has been done.

15. Deliverable state

Deliverable state has the same meaning under rule 2 as under rule 1 (13:**12**). The wording is otherwise interpreted straightforwardly —

Underwood v. *Burgh Castle Brick & Cement Syndicate* (1922): The subject of the sale was an engine weighing over 30 tons. It had sunk into its cement base due to its own weight. It was the seller's obligation to dismantle it and detach it from the floor. It was held that the engine was not in a deliverable state and so the property could not yet pass.

16. Notice to the buyer

Once the goods are in a deliverable state, the buyer must be notified. However, there is no stipulation that the seller must give notice of this fact, so a buyer could be informed of this by a third party.

17. Rule 3
This rule states that:

Where there is a contract for the sale of specific goods in a deliverable state but the seller is bound to weigh, measure, test or do some other act or thing with reference to the goods for the purpose of ascertaining the price, the property does not pass until the act or thing is done and the buyer has notice that it has been done.

18. Duty lies with the seller
Rule 3, like rule 2, applies when it is the *seller* who has to do something to the goods rather than the buyer (where rule 1 then applies) —

Turley v. *Bates* (1863): The contract for the sale of clay provided that the buyer had to weigh it in order to determine the price.
It was held that property has passed to the buyer when the contract was made.

19. Act must be to ascertain the price
In addition rule 3 *only* applies where the act is necessary to ascertain the price, not for some other purpose.

20. Notification
The buyer must be notified that the act has been carried out by the seller.
Rule 3 is illustrated by the following case —

Nanka Bruce v. *Commonwealth Trust Ltd* (1926): There was an agreement to sell cocoa at 90s per 60 lb. It was agreed that the buyer would re-sell the goods and that the sub-buyer would weigh them.
It was held that the property in the goods passed from the seller to the buyer *before* the sub-buyers had weighed them.

21. Rule 4
This rule states that:

. . . when goods are delivered to the buyer on approval or on sale or return or other similar terms, the property in the goods passes to the buyer:

(a) when he signifies his approval or acceptance to the seller or does any other act adopting the transaction;
(b) if he does not signify his approval or acceptance to the seller but retains the goods without giving notice of reflection, then, if a time has been fixed for the return of the goods, on the expiration of that time, and, if no time has been fixed, on the expiration of a reasonable time.

In such cases there is, initially, no contract of sale. One comes into existence only when the buyer shows an intention to purchase the goods or performs an act inconsistent with the seller's title.

22. Adoption of the goods
The buyer would adopt goods under rule 4(a) if he accepted offers for the goods, re-sold, pledged or otherwise dealt with the goods as though they were his own property —

Kirkham v. *Attenborough* (1897): The plaintiff gave goods to a customer on a sale or return basis. The customer pawned the goods. The plaintiff was never paid and so claimed the goods from the pawnbroker. It was held that he could not recover them because the pawning of the goods was an act adopting the transaction. Ownership passed to the customer as a result and he transferred it to the pawnbroker.

Also *see Weiner* v. *Gill* (1906).

23. Beyond control
If, however, the buyer is unable to return the goods within the approval period for a reason outside his control, e.g. theft, he will not be deemed to have adopted the transaction and so title to the goods will not pass.

24. Lapse of time
On the other hand, if the buyer does not signify his approval or acceptance to the seller, but retains the goods until after the goods should have been returned to the seller, then the buyer is deemed to have accepted the goods and ownership would therefore pass, under rule 4(b) —

Smiths Car Sales Ltd (1962): A seller left his car with the buyer for storage and authorised the buyer to sell the car if he could get £325 for it. After three months the seller demanded the return of the vehicle within three days or £325. The car was eventually returned some weeks later. It had been damaged by one of the buyer's employees when he had been using it for his own private purpose. The seller refused to accept the car and sued for the £325.

It was held that the buyer had retained the car beyond a reasonable time and therefore the property had passed under s. 18, rule 4(b), allowing the seller to sue for the price.

25. Rule 5

This section covers the passing of property in unascertained goods. Under this rule, unless a contrary intention is shown, where there is a contract for the sale of unascertained or future goods by description and the goods of that description, in a deliverable state, are apportioned unconditionally to the contract, then ownership will pass to the buyer. Rule 5 must be read together with s. 16 and it is also subject to a contrary intention appearing under s. 17.

26. Unconditional appropriation of the goods

The expression 'unconditional appropriation' is not defined in the Sale of Goods Act 1979, but is taken to mean instances where the seller or the buyer sets goods aside for performance of the contract. The buyer must assent to this before it can become effective —

D.F. Mount v. *Jay & Jay Ltd* (1960): Goods were apportioned under a contract by the seller. The buyer's assent was deemed to have been given by virtue of the buyer reselling the goods.

27. Deliverable state of the goods

Ownership cannot pass until the goods are in a deliverable state. Therefore, if the goods are delivered to a buyer mixed with others, ownership will not pass —

Healey v. *Howlett & Sons* (1917): It was held that ownership of a quantity of mackerel had not passed to the buyer because, although the seller had given the railway company (the carrier) instructions to *mark* 20 boxes of the mackerel for the buyer, the boxes had not been *separated* from the rest of the consignment and so had not been appropriated to the contract.

28. Assent is required

For the ownership of unascertained goods to pass to the buyer, not only must the goods be identified and appropriated to the contract by the seller or buyer, the other party must have assented to the appropriation. The courts have been reluctant to accept anything less than taking delivery of the goods as amounting to assent on the part of the buyer —

> *Carlos Federspial* v. *Charles Twigg Co.* (1957): It was held that the buyer had not affirmatively indicated his assent but merely not notified the seller of any objection.
> In this case, Pearson J. stated that risk passes from seller to buyer when the goods are shipped which normally means being delivered over the ship's rail.

29. Section 19

Section 19 deals with the area of reservation of the right in three sub-sections:

(a) *Section 19(1).* This states that even though the seller has appropriated the goods to the contract, he may reserve ownership of the goods until certain conditions are satisfied and/or until payment is made. This principle applies notwithstanding the delivery of the goods to the buyer. This means one can reserve the property of the goods by the terms of the contract or by appropriation of the contract.

(b) *Section 19(2).* This gives one specific example of the reservation of the right of disposal. If the seller takes out a Bill of Lading deliverable to his order, then this action presumes that the seller intends to keep the property in the goods. However, s. 19(2) is only prima facie and therefore can be rebutted by other evidence to the contrary.

(c) *Section 19(3).* This relates to where the seller has actually handed over the Bill of Lading to the buyer, along with the Bill of Exchange. By doing this, the seller implies that the buyer can have the document of title, for example the Bill of Lading, if he honours the Bill of Exchange. If the Bill of Exchange is dishonoured, the buyer must send back the Bill of Lading to the seller. Even if he does not return the Bill of Lading the property will not pass to him.

30. Retention of title clauses

Section 19 allows a seller to prevent ownership passing to the buyer by providing in the contract of sale that the seller shall retain the ownership of the goods until they are fully paid for. Various extensions to this clause can occur.

31. Time of reserving right of disposal

In the case of specific goods, the seller must reserve the right of disposal at the time the contract is made — *see Dannant* v. *Skinner & Collom* (1948). With others it can be done at the time of the contract or at the time of appropriation.

32. A safety net

Section 19 has been used to protect the interests of the seller in the event of the buyer becoming bankrupt. This enables him to have a claim on the *goods* rather than a *dividend*.

> *Aluminium Industries Vaasen BV* v. *Romalpa Ltd* (1976): The seller sold foil to Romalpa, an English company, for use in its manufacturing process. At the time of manufacture, the foil became mixed with other materials.
>
> A written contract contained a retention of title clause, under which ownership would be transferred when Romalpa had paid all sums owing to the seller. The clause went on to reserve ownership over any goods that were mixed with the aluminium foil.
>
> Romalpa became insolvent and a receiver was appointed. The seller claimed ownership of the foil still held by the company and the proceeds of the re-sale of unmixed foil sold by the receiver to third parties. No claim was made in respect of mixed goods or the proceeds of the sale of mixed goods.
>
> The Court of Appeal held that the retention of title clause was valid and the seller's claim succeeded in full.

The above case has been criticised as it enables a seller to have a secret form of security in the event of the buyer becoming bankrupt. The buyer's other creditors are therefore prejudiced by not knowing of this security. As a result, in *Re Bond Worth* (1980), Slade J. decided that such clauses should only reserve equitable rather than legal title to the goods. Also, in *Borden (UK) Ltd* v. *Scottish Timber Products* (1981) it was held that such a reservation had to be registered under the Companies Act 1985 in order to become effective, but this only applies where the buyer is a company.

This rule still applies and such charges registered are referred to as a floating charge. They are governed by s. 396(1)(f) of the Companies Act 1985 as amended by the Companies Act 1989, and require registration under s. 395. Some clauses that are slightly differently drafted have been regarded as a charge over book debts under s. 396(1)(e) — *see Re Weldtech Equipment Ltd* (1990) but to the same effect. Unregistered charges are void against the liquidator.

Section 19(2) presumes that title will pass in an international trade contract involving Bills of Lading when one has been transferred to the buyer and the price paid.

The rule from the Romalpa case (*ante*) has been used by sellers to reclaim unused leather in *Re Peachshort* (1983) and unused yarn in *Clough Mill Ltd* v. *Martin* (1984).

33. Section 20

Section 20 states that prima-facie risk passes with property, although in international contracts this has been displaced.

34. Strict f.o.b. contracts

Strict f.o.b. contracts do not involve the seller in the handling of the Bill of Lading so it has to be seen if there are any express provisions as to when property is to pass — *see The San Nicholas* (1976). The contract stated that the property was to pass when the goods passed the permanent hose connection of the ship.

If, however, there is no expression as to the intention of the parties, then s. 18, rule 5 has to be looked at. It states that the goods pass when they are unconditionally appropriated to the contract —

Federspiel v. *Twigg* (1957): An overseas buyer bought bicycles f.o.b. from a UK manufacturer and paid for them in advance. The manufacturer packed the bikes ready for export with the buyer's name just waiting for shipment. The manufacturer then went into liquidation.

It was held by Pearson J. that no property in the bikes had passed to the buyer. It was immaterial that the bikes had actually been set aside, duly packed for export with the buyer's name or that the seller had reserved the shipping space: ' . . . the last two acts to be performed by the seller, namely, sending the goods to Liverpool and having the goods shipped on board were not performed'. Property had not therefore yet passed to buyers as it had not yet been unconditionally appropriated. Although they had been appropriated to the contract, they could still have been withdrawn for another contract. Only when the bikes were put on board a vessel could there be unconditional appropriation as this was the last thing required of the f.o.b. buyer, which had not been performed. Property does not pass until this final act has been done.

35. Shipment to destination f.o.b.

There are divergent views as to when there is passing of property in these types of f.o.b., but the better view is that property passes on shipment in line with *Federspiel* v. *Twigg* (1957)(*ante*) as once the goods have been shipped, the Bill of Lading would be in the seller's possession for a while, but the seller here in the shipment to destination f.o.b. is the buyer's agent to arrange the carriage so the Bill of Lading may physically be in the seller's possession. Because the seller is the buyer's agent, then withholding the Bill of Lading would be a breach of the agency relationship.

36. Cost Insurance Freight contracts

In Cost Insurance Freight contracts, the Bill of Lading is important as the form in which it is drawn will show the seller's intention as to the passing of property, and, likewise, so will the seller's handling of the Bill of Lading.

Here the seller will take out a Bill of Lading deliverable to himself, i.e. to the seller's order. Section 19(2) of the Sale of Goods Act 1979 reinforces the presumption that the seller intends to keep the property in the goods. Even if the Bill of Lading makes the goods deliverable to the buyer's order, the fact that the seller retains the Bill of Lading in his possession may be an indication of his intention to retain the property —

> *The Kronprinsessan Margareta* (1921): The Bill of Lading was taken out to the buyer's order but the seller held on to the Bill of Lading so that the buyer could not achieve possession of the goods.
> It was held by the House of Lords that the property was still with the seller as retention of the Bill of Lading was inconsistent with the intention to pass property. Lord Sumner said in the case:

> It was clearly intended by the Consignor to preserve his title to the goods until he did a further act by transferring the Bill of Lading.

> This was called a 'price case' as it was common in the 1920s at a time of war to see if the goods belonged to the enemy or to friendly parties.

Cheetham v. *Thornham Spinning Co.* (1964): There was a Cost Insurance Freight contract for the sale of cotton Cost Insurance Freight Manchester, with payment to be in cash in exchange for the documents on arrival of the vessel. When the seller tendered the Bill of Lading, the buyer wanted to pay via a 90-day draft rather than by cash, so the seller did not hand the Bill of Lading over to the buyer but surrendered it instead to the carrier.

The seller authorised the carrier to release the goods to the buyer so that he could take them to his warehouse in order to save quay rent and other expenses. The buyer, however, disposed of the goods and went into liquidation.

It was held by Roskill J. that property in the goods did not pass and the seller was entitled to the full proceeds of the sale of these goods by the buyer as he still had title to the property of the goods.

According to s. 17 of the Sale of Goods Act 1979, the passing of property depends on the *intention* of the parties, so the fact that the seller at no time allowed the buyer to obtain the shipping documents evinced an intention to retain the property.

The latter case shows that the courts attach great significance to the fact that the seller held on to the Bill of Lading although he let the buyer have the goods as this was a clear signal of the seller's intent to keep the ownership.

37. The transfer of a Bill of Lading
However, where the seller transfers the Bill of Lading to the buyer, the ownership *still* may not pass as the general view is that the seller only *intends* property to pass if he receives payment —

Ginzberg v. *Barrow Haematite* (1966): The contract was for the sale of steel Cost Insurance Freight Birkenhead. The contract expressly provided for payment against documents. The vessel arrived before the Bill of Lading so an arrangement was made with the carrier to deliver the goods to the buyer against a ship's delivery order instead of a Bill of Lading, i.e. the contract was varied.

The buyer took delivery of the goods but did not pay as the company had been wound up. The seller sued for return of the goods or value of the goods as property had not passed.

It was held that the seller could claim the proceeds of the sale as property had not passed to the buyer; it was still the seller's property.

The effect of the modification of the contract, i.e. delivery against a delivery order instead of a Bill of Lading, was done to expedite delivery of the goods but it did not depart from the fundamental principles of a Cost Insurance Freight contract. There had not been unconditional appropriation of the goods to the buyer as the buyer had not paid cash against the documents as stated in the contract. Until payment had been made there could be no passing of property.

McNair J. in the case stated 'In Cost Insurance Freight contracts it is the parting with the Bill of Lading which is the last act to be performed by the seller'.

An example of a 'last act' can be seen in the following case —

The Albazero (1976): The first instance decision by Brandon J. in this case is very important. There was a contract for the sale of oil Cost Insurance Freight Antwerp. Both the seller and the buyer were subsidiaries of the same group of companies.

The oil was shipped and a Bill of Lading made the goods deliverable to the seller's order. The Bill of Lading stated that the vessel was to ' . . . proceed to Gibraltar for orders'. The shipping documents were sent to the carrier, a third subsidiary of the group in Paris. The carrier was acting as the seller's agent.

On 12 January, the carrier received the documents, endorsed the Bill of Lading and posted them to the buyer in Antwerp. On 13 January, the carrier, the seller's agent, posted the Bill of Lading to the buyer. On 14 January, the carrying vessel and cargo was totally lost. On 15 January, the buyer received the endorsed Bill of Lading and subsequently paid the seller for the cargo.

The issue in the case was whether property still remained with the seller at the time of the sinking or whether the property had already passed to the buyer.

It was held by Brandon J. that the loss of the right of disposal takes place as from the moment that the carrier dispatches the Bill of Lading to the buyer, even though the buyer may never receive the Bill of Lading.

It is not the constructive delivery of the documents that determines the passing of property but, rather, the loss of the right of disposal, which takes place as soon as the seller separates himself from the Bill of Lading by posting it. As from then, he has no power to dispose of the goods to some other buyer.

38. Ascertainment

Section 16 stresses that goods must be ascertained before passing of property can take place. Ascertainment can take place by deletion or by selection —

> *The Elafi* (1981): There were a number of contracts for the same type of goods and various lots were shipped under different Bills of Lading. Some cargo was to be discharged at Rotterdam, the rest at Hamburg. The Rotterdam cargo was discharged from the vessel there and then it went on to Hamburg. After its arrival at Hamburg but before the discharging of the goods, the cargo was damaged.
> The buyer claimed against the carrier for the damage to the goods under s. 1 of the Bills of Lading Act 1855 and said that property had passed by virtue of the endorsement of the Bills of Lading. They also brought an action in tort.
> It was held that the buyer had the property in the goods and that the property had passed to the buyer because all the goods on board were his at Hamburg. Also, the last necessary act required for the property to pass was for the goods to be ascertained. This was done by the deletion of the other goods at the earlier ports.
> The Bill of Lading had already been passed to the buyer prior to the damage and, therefore, the goods were ascertained, so the buyer could sue the carrier in tort. Here there was ascertainment of the goods by deletion.

39. Documentary credits

If a documentary credit system is used instead, then the position will be more straightforward as property will pass when the seller hands over the documents to the bank, which acts as an agent for the buyer. In this way, the issue of reservation of rights is avoided —

> *Sale Continuation* v. *Austin Taylor* (1968): stated that 'the seller parts with ownership when he sends the documents to the bank'. This means that once there is a letter of credit, property cannot be retained by the seller once the Bill of Lading has been handed over to the bank.

Progress test 13

1. What are the main reasons for wanting to know when the property in goods has passed? **(1)**

2. What is the effect of s. 16 of the Sale of Goods Act 1979? **(2)**

3. What are unascertained goods? **(2)**

4. What is the difference between unascertained and mixed goods? **(2, 3)**

5. What is a *Romalpa* clause? **(4, 29, 30)**

6. What are the rules for ascertaining unascertained goods? **(4, 5)**

7. What are *specific* goods? **(6, 11)**

8. What is the effect of s. 17 of the Sale of Goods Act 1979? **(6, 7)**

9. What are the guidelines for trying to find the intention of parties to a contract? **(7, 8)**

10. Why is s. 18 of the Sale of Goods Act so important? **(11–21)**

14
Incoterms

Introduction

1. Background

Incoterms have been widely used since 1936 in international trade transactions. The present 1990 edition has 13 terms arranged in 4 groups. It is quite common for parties in contracts to specify certain duties as being according to the 1990 Incoterms.

2. What are Incoterms?

Incoterms are international commercial terms that are used in business mainly to make clear the delivery obligations of each contracted party. The 1990 edition is presented in a logical order, making it easier to understand than previous editions. New terms have been included to take into account current developments, e.g. replacing 'documents' with 'electronic data' as most businesses tend to communicate electronically. Also, new developments in transport-ation have been taken into account.

The obligations and rights of both buyer and seller under Cost Insurance Freight contracts as well as being defined over time through numerous Common Law decisions are also specified in the Incoterms — a list in a document published by the International Chamber of Commerce.

The list comprises a set of international rules for the interpretation of trade terms. The 1990 edition is presently in use and referred to as the 1990 Incoterms.

Should businesses wish to use these Incoterms to interpret the contract in which they are involved, then a clause must be included to this effect — *The Albazero* (1975) (13:**37**). In many countries, Incoterms actually have a statutory effect or are viewed as part of the custom of the trade. This is not yet so within the United Kingdom, despite their being in existence since 1936.

There are ten main obligations under the 1990 Incoterms that apply to both buyer and seller, although not all obligations are applicable to each contract.

Use of Incoterms

3.　Interpretation

It is important to be able to interpret a trade term properly in order to ascertain the detailed obligations of buyer and seller. For example, Cost Insurance Freight only indicates that goods should be delivered in a usual manner and that the buyer pays the cost of carriage, etc., but does not make clear matters such as risk of loss or damage to the goods. Such terms were traditionally defined under the various Sale of Goods Acts, but more recently the task has been taken on by organisations such as the International Chamber of Commerce.

4.　Incorporation of Incoterms into a contract of sale

This is done in the following way: After the main provisions of the contract have been specified, or expressly requested by the buyer or seller, a clause may be added to the contract, e.g. the contract of sale could specify what the property rights of the respective parties are but imply Incoterms 1990 in relation to matters concerning the risk factor. The contract would also make specific provisions for consequences of breaches as they are not dealt with under Incoterms.

5.　Divisions

The 1990 Incoterms fall into four main component groups, listed as C, D, E and F. Each group has important differences from the next that are best highlighted when goods become damaged in transit. The concerns of each group are described next.

6.　Group C

Group C terms include the following:

(a)　cost and freight (CFR);
(b)　cost, insurance and freight (CIF);
(c)　carriage paid to (CPT);
(d)　carriage and insurance paid to (CIP).

C terms extend the seller's obligation with respect to carriage costs and insurance to the destination. Under such terms, the seller has totally fulfilled his delivery obligation even if something should happen to the goods post-shipment. For example, if goods should be lost in transit, the seller would not be liable for breach of contract and would not therefore need to provide substitute goods. The C terms therefore make clear that a seller fulfils all obligations once the goods have been handed over for shipment; obligations do not extend to destinations (this is covered by the D terms).

7. Group D

Group D terms include the following:

(a) delivered at frontier (DAF);
(b) delivered ex ship (DES);
(c) delivered ex quay (DEQ);
(d) delivered duty unpaid (DDU);
(e) delivered duty paid (DDP).

D terms extend the seller's obligations regarding delivery to beyond the destination point, so should goods be damaged in transit, the seller having sold under D terms would be liable to substitute the goods.

Sometimes C and D terms may appear similar but, in fact, they are very different. A seller choosing a D term must have a clear clause saying so included in the contract of sale.

D terms are quite a popular choice in international trade contracts but the main factors to be borne in mind when choosing from the different D terms are the mode of transport to be used, how the risks and costs are to be distributed and clearance of goods for import.

8. DDU

DDU is a new addition to the 1990 Incoterms and, under this term, it is the buyer's duty to clear the goods for import — all arrangements to be made at his risk and expense.

9. Group E

Group E terms only consist of ex works (EXW).

Under this term, the seller's obligation is only to make the goods available at his premises; there is no duty for the seller to arrange for export of the goods — this is the buyer's obligation. The seller need only assist, if necessary.

10. Group F

Group F terms include the following:

(a) free carrier (FCA);

(b) free alongside ship (FAS);
(c) free on board (FOB).

Under F terms, the seller's obligation is to arrange for all pre-carriage facilities prior to the goods being handed over to the carrier for carriage to the buyer's destination. The main carriage arrangements are to be handled by the buyer.

11. CIF and FOB

The obligations of the parties to a CIF or FOB contract have been listed in the 1990 Incoterms. They differ slightly from the Common Law decisions discussed in previous chapters.

12. CIF — the seller's main duties

As given in the Group C terms in the 1990 Incoterms, for CIF, the seller's primary duties are, first, to contract the usual terms used for the transport system being used. This is to be at his total expense and covers carriage of the goods right up to the destination point.

Second, the seller has to obtain, at his own expense, cargo insurance as agreed in the contract. The seller need only have the minimum cover required, but it is for the buyer to specify any extended cover that may be required. This extension will be at the buyer's expense. The duration of the insurance cover must be from shipment to the agreed port of destination.

The seller must also:

(a) supply contract conforming goods;
(b) deliver goods on board ship;
(c) load goods and pay the costs incurred for loading or unloading;
(d) furnish a clean Bill of Lading, invoice and insurance policy for the goods shipped to the buyer (these documents may be replaced by electronic data messages).

13. CIF — the buyer's main duties

Also as specified in the Group C terms in the 1990 Incoterms, for CIF, the buyer's primary duties are to pay all costs incurred in obtaining the Bill of Lading, insurance documents, etc. and to reimburse the seller if needs be. Also, the buyer, upon request, must provide any information needed to obtain an insurance policy. The seller need only obtain minimum insurance so the buyer must make clear any additional cover that is required and pay for it.

The buyer must also:

(a) accept delivery of the goods;

(b) accept the documents tendered;
(c) pay the price against the documents received;
(d) pay any unloading costs not included in the general freight charges.

14. FOB — the seller's main duties

As given in the Group F terms in the 1990 Incoterms, for FOB, the seller's primary duties are, first, to provide contract conforming goods and to keep evidence of such and, second, to invoice the buyer for such contract conforming goods provided. Importantly, the seller has to obtain any export licence or other authorisation needed to export the goods — paying all expenses involved in doing this.

Further, the seller must place the contract conforming goods on board the ship within the time limit agreed with the buyer. Risk is then transferred to the buyer. The seller then has the duty of giving the buyer sufficient notice that goods have been delivered on board the ship named, within the time specified, as requested by the buyer.

The seller must also:

(a) pay the costs of checking operations involved in delivery of the goods (i.e. loading costs);
(b) assist the buyer in obtaining a Bill of Lading and any other documents.

15. FOB — the buyer's main duties

Also as specified in the Group F terms in the 1990 Incoterms, for FOB, the buyer's primary duties are to pay the contract price to the seller, arrange for any import licences needed (as the seller does for the export licence), and pay all the expenses incurred.

The buyer must also take delivery of the goods once they have been put on board ship and any risk of loss or damage is transferred from the seller to the buyer after reaching the delivery point. It is important that the buyer notifies the seller of the name of the vessel, loading place and required delivery time. Any additional costs incurred by the seller as a result of the buyer's failure to do so must be reimbursed by the buyer. Further, the buyer must pay for the seller's assistance in obtaining documents or electronic messages.

Progress test 14

1. What are Incoterms and what part do they play in international trade? **(1–4)**

2.   How are Incoterms integrated with provisions of a contract?
(4)

3.   Do the Incoterms have any statutory effect within the UK?
(5)

4.   What are the main divisions?   **(6–10)**

5.   What are the seller's and buyer's duties for CIF contracts under Incoterms?   **(12, 13)**

6.   What are the seller's and buyer's main duties for an f.o.b. contract under Incoterms?   **(14, 15)**

15
Marine insurance

Introduction

1. **The basic principles of insurance**
    These are:

(a) utmost good faith;
(b) indemnity;
(c) insurable interest.

Marine Insurance Act 1906

2. **Misrepresentation and representation**
Under the normal law of contract, silence does not amount to misrepresentation. However, in insurance law this assumption is reversed — it is assumed that the proposer knows *everything* relevant to the risk and that the insurer knows *nothing* or virtually nothing. Thus, the obligation of full disclosure falls squarely upon the proposer.

3. **Section 17**
    This is a broad section but it is not very helpful. A contract of marine insurance is one based on the utmost good faith, and, if the utmost good faith is not observed by either party, the contract may be avoided by the other party.

4. **Section 18**
    This is where the proposer becomes the assured.

5. **Section 18(1)**
    Here the assured must disclose to the insurer, before the contract is concluded, every material circumstance known to the assured and he is deemed to know every circumstance that, in the ordinary course

of business, ought to be known by him. If the assured fails to make such a disclosure, the insurer may avoid the contract.

NOTE: Section 18(1) only relates to events before the conclusion of the contract. This section also has a deeming provision whereby the assured is deemed to know certain things.

6.   Section 18(2)

It is taken that every circumstance is material which would influence the judgement of a prudent insurer in fixing the premium or determining whether or not to accept the risk:

(a) here the definition of material circumstance is related to its necessity to the prudent insurer under the reasonable man test, i.e. it is objective;

(b) it is a double-barrelled test:
(*i*)   whether the prudent insurer would take the risk;
(*ii*)   if he would, then he would have to consider the premium that he would charge for taking it.

7.   Section 18(3)

The following do *not* have to be disclosed:

(a) *Section 18(3)(a)*. Any circumstance that diminishes the risk.

(b) *Section 18(3)(b)*. A counter deeming provision. Any circumstance that is known or presumed to be known to the *insurer*. The insurer is presumed to know of matters of common notoriety or knowledge and matters which an insurer in the ordinary course of his business, as such, ought to know —

North British Fishing Boat Insurance v. *Stan* (1922): Here there was an insurer/re-insurer relationship. The plaintiff was an insurer who had re-insured a risk with the defendant. The risk in question concerned a ship that had been destroyed by fire — a peril the owner had insured against.
The re-insurer said that the policy was avoidable by reason of non-disclosure of the facts that:

(a) in the previous year there had been an exceptional increase in the number and severity of the fire losses coming from boats insured by the plaintiff.
(b) another firm (State Insurance Company) with which the plaintiff had been placing the re-insurance risk since 1914 had refused to accept the re-insurance in 1921 (the year in question).

It was held that there was no obligation to make the disclosure of (b). Also, although (a) was a material circumstance within the meaning of s. 18, the assured did not need to have disclosed it because that particular increase was such as a prudent insurer would know in the ordinary course of his business (i.e. s. 18(3)(b) comes into play).

(c) *Section 18(3)(c).* Any circumstance information about which is waived by the insurer.
(d) *Section 18(3)(d).* Any circumstance that it is superfluous to disclose by reason of any expressed or implied warranty.

8. Section 19

This concerns the obligation of disclosure that rests on the agent/broker.

Where insurance is effected for the assured by an agent, the agent must disclose to the insurer:

(a) *Section 19(a).* Every material circumstance known to himself, and an agent is deemed to know every circumstance that, in the ordinary course of business, ought to be known by or have been communicated to him. This part also has a deeming provision.
(b) *Section 19(b).* Every material circumstance that the assured is bound to disclose, unless it comes to his knowledge too late to communicate it to the agent. This can be a very harsh principle in practice —

> *Anglo-African Merchants* v. *Bayley* (1970): The assured asked Bayley to insure some bales of unused government surplus jerkins. In placing the risk, Bayley described the goods to underwriters as '. . . new men's clothes in bales'. They were later stolen. A claim was made under the insurance that was rejected by the insurer.
> It was held that the insurer could avoid the contract by reason of non-disclosure, i.e. by the wrongful description of the goods.

9. Summary

In relation to marine insurance, the insurer's duty is, therefore, one of utmost good faith — *see Carter* v. *Boehm* (1766) for Mansfield L.J.'s classic statement on this point. This duty is, however, mutual in that it applies to *both* parties within the contract. This was reinforced in the case of *Bank of Nova Scotia* v. *Hellenic Mutual War Risks Association* (1989), otherwise known as the Good Luck case.

There was failure on the part of the insurers to disclose that the insurance policy was avoidable for non-disclosure. In arriving at their decision, the courts referred to the case of *Banque Financière de la Cité SA* v. *Westgate Insurance Company* (1989).

If it is the insured party that fails to disclose a material fact, then the contract can be avoided but damages are not usually available unless it is the insurer who is liable.

Held covered clauses

10. Past and present

In the three sets of Institute cargo clauses — A, B and C — that were in operation until 1982, the assured was held to be covered at a premium to be arranged with regard to misdescriptions of the goods, the voyage, etc. However, since 1983 and under the present standard ABC clauses, held covered clauses are no longer included.

11. Clause 10

The change of voyage clause used to include holding cover for a change of voyage and a misdescription of the goods. However, now the old utmost good faith principle has reasserted itself so that presently one is only covered for change of voyage, not for misdescription.

12. Held covered clauses in court

These clauses did not always keep the insurance in force —

Hewitt Bros v. *Wilson* (1915): Insurance was effected on three cases of machinery; two were new and one was secondhand. All three cases were lost through the operation of one of the insured's perils. The insurer tried to avoid the claim, saying that the insurance company was not told that two were new and one was secondhand and, thus, they had made a contract for three new cases.
It was held that the misrepresentation in the form of the non-disclosure, although material, was innocent and so the insurer was liable under the policy.
Thus, here, the held covered clause kept the policy in operation and kept the insurer from avoiding the policy.

Overseas Commodities v. *Style* (1958): The insurance related to tins of pork shipped from France to the UK. In placing the insurance, the assured stated that all the tins were marked

with the manufacturer's dating code. However, he *knew* that
they had not, in fact, been stamped.
When the tins of pork arrived in the UK, the Health Authority
seized the tins as they could not be sold without a stamp. The
assured then claimed under the policy.
It was held that the held covered clause would not serve to
keep the insurance in force because the assured did not act
innocently, but instead fraudulently misrepresented the goods.

This principle is designed to prevent the assured profiting from the
insurance. The insurance is to provide indemnity or compensation
for a loss, but no more.

Subrogation

13. Subrogation and the Marine Insurance Act 1969
Subrogation is governed by s. 79 of the Act:

(a) *Section 79(1).* Where the insurer pays for a *total loss* either of the
whole or, in the case of goods, any apportionable part of the sum
insured, *he thereupon becomes entitled, not required, to take over the interest*
of the assured in whatever may remain of the sum so paid for, and
he is thereby subrogated to all the rights and remedies of the assured
in and in respect of that sum as from the time of the casualty causing
the loss.

(b) *Section 79(2).* Where the insurer pays for a partial loss, he acquires
no title to the sum insured, or such part of it as may remain, but he
is thereupon subrogated to all rights and remedies of the assured in
and in respect of the sum insured from the time of the casualty
causing the loss, in so far as the assured has been indemnified by such
payment for the loss.

14. Subrogation in practice
This means that, in the event of an insurer paying a claim in
circumstances where the loss was occasioned by a third party in an
actionable way to the extent of the payment under the policy, the
right against the third party which initially existed in the assured
would be transferred to the insurer, i.e. the insurer would be
subrogated to the rights that mutually existed in the assured.

Thus, subrogation equals the transfer of rights from the assured
to the insurer by means of some third party. If there is no third party,
however, subrogation has no rights to transfer, so a third party would
be needed —

Goole & Hull Steam Towing Co. v. *Ocean Marine Insurance* (1927): A ship was insured for £4000. It was involved in a collision and the necessary repairs to the ship cost £5000. It was agreed that both parties were at fault in causing the collision. X paid the shipowner £2500, representing his 50 per cent share of the damage suffered. The shipowner then claimed against the insurers for an additional £2500, but the insurers refused the claim.

It was held that the shipowner was only entitled to £1500 by operation of the policy of subrogation by analogy.

The traditional sequence of events in subrogation is:

(a) collision;
(b) the assured claims against the insurer;
(c) the insurer claims against the third party by exercising its right of subrogation.

In *Goole*, there was (a) and (b), but, instead of (c), the assured claimed against the insurer. It was held that there should be no difference in the result despite the different sequence of events.

This, therefore, is a legal technique for avoiding the possibility of the assured profiting from the insurance —

Lucas v. *ECGD* (1974): The insurer was the ECGD under one of their policies. They exported to Egypt and sterling was devalued. This resulted in an amount of money being received by the Egyptian party that was greater than the amount paid out by the ECGD. Who was entitled to the windfall?

It was held that the insured, i.e. Lucas, was entitled to the surplus on the wording of a clause in the contract.

A.G. v. *The Glen Line* (1930): The ship, The Glen Line, arrived in Germany on 15 July 1914. After it had discharged its cargo, it was prevented from leaving by the German authorities as World War I had broken out and the ship was detained in Germany until the end of the war.

In less than one year after the detention began, the shipowner decided to give a notice of abandonment to its insurers. The insurers paid £61000.

In 1918, the ship was returned to the insurers and then sold off for £160 000 — out of which sum they had to pay 80 per cent to the British government as re-insurers of the ship.

Under the Treaty of Versailles 1920, provisional

compensation was awarded for the property of foreign nationals that had been in Germany on 1 August 1914. The shipowner presented the claim for loss of earnings caused by the acts of the German authorities of retaining the ship to a mixed arbitral tribunal. £136 000 was then paid to the ship. The Board of Trade said that the amount belonged to themselves and the insurers and split the money 80 per cent to A.G. and 20 per cent to the insurers, by reason of the abandonment of the ship as a constructive total loss. The insurers disagreed.

It was held that neither the A.G. nor the insurers were entitled to any of the amounts paid by Germany relating to the loss of profits.

Yorkshire Insurance Company v. *Nisbett* (1961): The assured owned a ship that was involved in a collision with a Canadian government ship. The assured's ship was a total loss. The insurers paid out $72 000 for the loss. The Canadian government's ship was entirely to blame so subrogation rights arose with the insurer *vis à vis* the Canadian government, who were slow to pay out.

In 1949, between the time of collision and the time of paying out, sterling was devalued relative to the Canadian dollar so that when the $72 000 was converted, it was equal to £120 000. Who should keep the difference?

It was held that the assured was entitled to retain the difference. Thus, here subrogation was tightened, limiting the position of the assured with regard to payment arising by reason of the insurance, not for extra amounts that arose other than reasons besides insurance, e.g. fluctuation of the sterling against the Canadian dollar.

If Nisbett had been uninsured and the same thing had happened, he would still have ended up with £120 000 as the extra amount arose as a result of factors outside the insurance, i.e. it arose because of the devaluation of the dollar so it could not be retained by the insurer.

Insurable interest

15. Insurable interest and the Marine Insurance Act 1906

Insurable interest is governed by ss. 4–6 of the Act, especially ss. 4 and 5 (for the assured to have a valid contract of insurance, he must have an insurance interest in the sum insured):

(a) *Section 4(1)*. This is a broad statement of policy. Every contract of marine insurance is deemed to be a gaming/wagering contract.
(b) *Section 4(2)*. This defines what kinds of marine insurance are gaming/wagering.
(c) *Section 4(2)(2)*. This concerns those cases where the assured does not have an insurance interest as defined by this Act and the contract is entered into with no expectation of acquiring such an interest. In short, when there is no insurance interest.
(d) *Section 4(2)(b)*. This concerns PP1 policies, where the policy is made 'interest or no interest' or without further proof of interest than the policy itself or without benefit of salvage to the insurer or subject to any other like term.

16. Definition of insurable interest
It is defined by s. 5 of the Marine Insurance Act 1906:

(a) *Section 5(1)*. Every person has an insurable interest who is involved in a marine venture.
(b) *Section 5(2)*. This section states that insurable interest when there is some connection between the assured and the property in question, i.e. when the assured stands to benefit/lose from its loss/obstruction.

Contribution

17. Contribution's purpose
Contribution is to be found in s. 32 of the Marine Insurance Act 1969; it is designed to avoid the assured claiming and being paid more than once for a loss if he is insured with more than one insurer.

Only a pro rata amount is to be paid out by the insurer. This way the assured is indemnified for the loss but does not benefit from it any more than that.

The contract of marine insurance

18. Marine insurance and marine policy
Section 22 of the Marine Insurance Act 1906 states that a contract of marine insurance is inadmissible in evidence unless it is embodied in a marine policy, which means it must be reduced to the form of a policy.

19. Warranties

These are additional terms on a contract of marine insurance and are dealt with in s. 33 of the 1906 Act.

Section 33(1) states that 'warranty' in these circumstances means a promissory warranty, i.e. a warranty that something will or will not be done. Section 33(2) goes on to state that a warranty may be expressed or implied. Expressed warranties are frequently used in policies, say, in describing a ship, e.g. that the ship is not to be older than X years.

Section 33(3) states that a warranty is a condition-type term that must be complied with exactly. It if is not complied with then the insurer will be discharged from liability as from the date of the breach of warranty.

Under the Marine Insurance Act 1906, there are certain warranties that can be contracted out of, the most important of which is given in s. 39. The section creates an implied warranty that, at the commencement of the voyage, the ship is seaworthy — 'seaworthy' being a relative term depending on the voyage in question.

However, s. 39 can be contracted out of by means of clause 5 of the Institute of Cargo Clauses (ICC), unless the insurer is privy to the unseaworthiness of the vessel.

Clause 5(1) states that in no case shall this insurance cover any loss, damage or expense arising from:

(a) unseaworthiness of the vessel or craft;
(b) unfitness of the vessel, craft, conveyance or container;

where the assured or those in his employ are privy to such unseaworthiness of unfitness at the time the shipmaster insured is installed.

However, clause 5(5) allows the underwriters to waiver any breach of the implied warranties of seaworthiness and fitness of the ship to carry the subject matter insured to the destination *unless* the assured or those in his employ are privy to such unseaworthiness or unfitness.

It is therefore possible to contract out of s. 39 of the Act using clause 5 of the ICCs *except* where the insurer is privy to the unseaworthiness and fitness of the vessel.

Types of marine insurance policy

20. The main types of policy

The main types of marine insurance policy are:

(a) facultative, floating and open covers;
(b) valued and unvalued policies;
(c) voyage and time policies.

A description of each of these now follows, together with some of their main features.

21. Facultative insurance, floating policies and open covers
The main features of each of these are as follows:

(a) *Facultative policies.* Here the insurance is placed on a one-off basis, i.e. it is an individual, one-off insurance policy to cover a particular shipment. An infrequent shipper of goods will insure under a facultative policy, for example.

(b) *Floating policies.* Here the assured takes out a fixed amount of insurance as specified in s. 29 of the Marine Insurance Act 1906. As the goods are shipped, the assured completes a declaration form that is then sent off to the insurer. In return, the insurer will issue a certificate of insurance relating to that particular insurance. With floating policies, the premium on the entirety of the coverage is paid at the onset.

(c) *Open cover policies.* These are more widely used than floating policies. Here a blanket insurance is arranged beforehand on a time basis, e.g. 12 months, rather than on a fixed money amount. No policy is issued at the outset so no premium has to be paid at the outset. However, s. 22 of the Act states that a marine insurance contract cannot be enforced without a policy so, in theory, the defect of an open cover policy is that it is not enforceable.

An advantage of this type of policy is that it is easier to keep a track of items, which is helpful in terms of administration.

22. Payment of premiums
The usual practice under open cover policies is for declarations to be accumulated on a monthly basis. The assured will then be billed for the premiums that have accrued. Thus, the availability of insurance and the payment for the insurance coincide.

23. Common features of floating and open cover policies
These include:

(a) *A classification clause.* This limits the kinds of ships on which the goods can be carried. For example it may specify for goods to be shipped on vessels of a certain standard such as that the ships be made of steel, mechanically propelled, etc.

(b) *A cancellation clause*. This can be used to cancel the cover on a certain number of days' notice. It only applies to new shipments, so if goods have already been shipped, the insurer cannot cancel the cover, he can only cancel future shipments. By means of such a clause, an insurer can get out of the long-term obligations he has entered into.

(c) *Risk spreading*. There is the assumption that a degree of risk spreading will be involved. For example, a £10 million floating policy will not be for one shipment valued at £10 million, as it would be under a facultative policy.

24. Common limits
These include:

(a) *A limit per bottom clause*. This limits the amount of goods that can be insured on one ship at any one time. If the insured wanted to go beyond this he would have to have the larger amount authorised by the underwriters, who might charge an extra premium for this. If such authorisation is not obtained, a breach of the limit means that the excess will not be covered.

(b) *A limit per location clause*. This states that not more than £X of insured goods (of which he has control) are to be found at the assured's location at any time. Such clauses only apply to the origin end of the journey, not to instances of trans-shipment to the destination of the journey as these locations will not be under the control of the assured if, say, a strike situation occurs there.

Limit per bottom and limit per location clauses require that all goods shipped by the assured that fall under the terms of the arrangement be declared. This duty of disclosure ends when the contract is concluded, i.e. when the floating policy or open cover is taken out — see *La Point* (1986). This disclosure duty is intended to control the risk, which is the basis on which the premium is set.

25. Valued and unvalued policies
With these types of policy, the sum insured is the total of all the subscriptions of the various underwriters, i.e. the maximum amount payable under the policy. The insurable value is the value of the thing insured. The essential features of the two types are:

(a) *A valued policy*. This type of policy is covered by s. 27 of the Marine Insurance Act 1906. Here the insurable value has been determined from the outset. If a loss occurs, the insurers will pay out the agreed sum, i.e. it would not be necessary to quantify the loss.

(b) *An unvalued policy.* This type of policy is covered by s. 28 of the Act. Here the insurable value is left open, being determined *after* a loss occurs, i.e. at the time of the claim as there is no prior agreement on the value. Section 16 of the Act sets out how to determine the insurable value of the subject matter.

26. Voyage and time policies

The main features of these two types of policy are as follows:

(a) *A voyage policy.* Under this policy, the contract is to insure the subject matter 'at and from', or, from one place to another or others.

(b) *A time policy.* Under this policy, the contract is to insure the subject matter for a definite period of time.

Hull voyages are usually insured with a time policy whereas cargo voyages are usually insured with a voyage policy. Both types are regulated by s. 25 of the Marine Insurance Act 1906.

This section also states that a contract for both voyage and time cover may be included in the same policy. This is called a *hybrid policy* —

> *Silver Dolphin Products* v. *Parcel & General Assurance* (1984): On 14 January, the goods were shipped from New York to London. The f.o.b. buyer asked their forwarding agents to arrange the insurance cover after shipment took place.
> On 19 January, the shipment was declared to the insurers under an open cover policy. The certificate of insurance that was issued had printed on it 'Voyage, 19 January at sea'. Unknown to anyone, the goods were already lost at that time (19 January). The issue was as to when the insurer's liability began.
> The court held that it was a hybrid contract so, although it covered the voyage from New York to London, the time limit was as from 19 January. Therefore, the insurer was *not* liable for loss prior to that date.

Section 42 of the Marine Insurance Act 1906 states that where the shipmaster is insured on a voyage policy, it is not necessary that the ship be at that place when the contract is concluded, but there is an implied condition that the voyage will commence within a written time. If not, the insurer can avoid the contract. Thus, under s. 42, the voyage must commence within a written time for the insurers to be able to avoid liability.

There are certain circumstances outlined in ss. 43 and 44 of the

Act when the insurers will not be liable for the risk, or, the risk will not 'attach'.

27. Non-attachment of risk

Where the place of departure is specified by the policy and the ship, instead of sailing from that place, sails from another place, the risk does not attach, i.e. if a ship starts from the wrong place heading for the right place, no risk attaches. Such alteration of the port of departure is covered in s. 43 of the Marine Insurance Act 1906.

Similarly, s. 44 states that where the destination is specified in the policy and the ship, instead of sailing for that destination, sails to another destination, the risk does not attach, i.e. where the ship starts from the right place but sails to the wrong place, risk does not attach —

> *George Kallis* v. *Success Insurance* (1985): The voyage insured was from Hong Kong to Cyprus but this voyage never took place.
> It was held that the risk did not attach.

Once the risk has attached, then ss. 45 and 46 come into play.

28. Change of voyage

Under s. 45, if the vessel sails from its agreed departure port to the agreed arrival port but, after commencement of the risk, the destination is voluntarily changed from the destination in the policy, then there is a *change of voyage*.

Where there is a change of voyage, the insurer is discharged from liability in accordance with s. 45(2). This is effective as from the time of the change, i.e. from the time that the determination to change is manifested.

29. Deviation

Section 26(2) of the Marine Insurance Act 1906 defines deviation as occurring:

(a) where the course of the voyage is specifically designated by the policy and that course is departed from;
(b) where the course of the voyage is not specifically designated by the policy, but the usual and customary course is departed from.

Section 46(1) of the Act lays down what is to happen when deviation occurs. If a route has been specifically designated, but the ship departs or deviates from it without lawful excuse, the insurer will be discharged from any liability from the time the deviation begins. It is immaterial that the ship may have regained her route before any loss occurs.

However, s. 46 can be contracted out of by means of clause 8(3) of the ICCs. This clause states that the insurer shall remain in force during any delay to the voyage which is beyond the control of the assured (s. 48), any deviation (s. 46), forced discharge, re-shipment or trans-shipment will be an offence, therefore cl. 8(3) can waive s. 46. Also during any variation of the venture arising from the exercise of a liberty granted to shipowners or charterers under the contract of affreignment will allow the innocent party to bring an action.

Section 49 allows deviation to be excused under certain circumstances, one of which is delay (s. 48).

30. Delay

If there is a delay without lawful excuse, the insurer is discharged from liability as from the time when the delay becomes unreasonable. This is laid down in s. 48. However, s. 48 can also be contracted out of using the ICCs clause 8(3).

31. Trans-shipment

There is no clause in the Marine Insurance Act 1906 prohibiting trans-shipment even though the Common Law position was that unless trans-shipment could be justified by disasters *en route* it would be considered to amount to a deviation.

Section 59 of the Act states what the effect of trans-shipment is, which is that the liability of the insurer will continue notwithstanding the trans-shipment whereby a peril insured against the voyage is avoided. However, trans-shipment *must* be brought about by a peril covered by the insurer, otherwise the cover will cease and the goods will not be covered.

There are three stages to determining the effect of trans-shipment:

(a) Stage 1: policy on risk;
(b) Stage 2: causal link;
(c) Stage 3: exemptions.

These are now described.

32. Policy on risk

Stage 1 is to consider whether at the time or place of a loss, the policy was irrevocably on risk. The ICCs clause 8 is the more relevant here of their clauses. Clause 8 is the warehouse or transit clause and defines the starting and stopping occasions to the policy being on risk.

Clause 8(1) states that the insurance attaches from the time the goods leave the warehouse or place of storage for commencement of the transit and continues during the ordinary course of transit. The insurance does, however, terminate on delivery to the consignees, final warehouse, etc., at the destination or other final warehouse, which is usually the first stop on the way to the final destination.

Clauses 8(1)(2), and 8(1)(2)(1) suggest that there should be a process that will take place at the first stop, that the goods are not just there to rest, e.g. relabelling, repackaging, etc.

Clause 8(1)(3) gives a 60-day limit that begins at the time of unloading, which means that after the 60 days the policy goes off risk. In stage 1 it can be said that the starting point in trans-shipment usually causes no problems, but the stopping point is often ambiguous and gives rise to difficulty.

33. Causal link

In stage 2, one has to consider whether there is the necessary degree of causal link between a risk insured against and the loss suffered.

Under s. 55 of the Marine Insurance Act 1906, there must be a loss caused by a peril that has been insured against, but, under the ICCs clauses (B), the loss must be written 'attributable to Institute of Cargo Clauses (B) policy', which at first glance lowers the level of the necessary connection needed between the occurrence of the risk and the occurrence of the loss. Clause 1(2) of (B), however, phrases loss of or damage to the sum insured as 'caused by'. The words 'caused by' suggest that a higher standard of causal link, as in s. 55, is needed.

Under the old ICCs, the peril of the sea risk used to include collision and this is still provided for, now under the ICCs clause 1(1)(4): '. . . collision or contact of vessel craft or conveyance with any external object other than water'.

However, under the old ICCs there was a heavy weather clause, but there is now no equivalent in (B)- and (C)- type policies.

Also, under the old ICCs the peril of the sea clause used to include some thefts. This is no longer so, however, unless the risk of theft is written in specifically at the time of conclusion of the contract as an additional peril to be insured against. Otherwise, goods that have been stolen are no longer covered.

On the other hand, there are some risks that the old ICCs never used to cover. For example, under the ICCs clause (1)(1)(3) of (B), there is specific mention of overturning or derailment of land conveyance, which were not included before.

As we have seen, heavy weather is no longer included. Previously, if this caused water to enter the vessel and damage was caused, this was taken to be a peril of the sea. Now, the ICCs clause 1(23) of (B) has broadened this concept so that, now it does not matter *how* the water got in as long as it is in the nature of rising water, not falling water as it does not cover rain.

There are some risks that are covered under the ICCs (B) policy that are not under the (C) policy:

(a) clause 1(1)(6) covers earthquake, volcanic eruption or lightning;

(b) clause 1(2)(2) covers washing overboard;

(c) clause 1(2)(3) covers the entry of sea, lake or river water;

(d) clause 1(3) covers the total loss of any package that has fallen overboard.

The burden of establishing that the loss was occasioned by the operation of a certain risk falls squarely on the assured —

The Popi M. (1985): The ship sprang a leak and then flooded. Three out of five cargo holds were also flooded. The shipmaster abandoned the ship together with his crew and the ship later sank.

It had to be shown that the loss was due to a peril of the sea, but no good explanation was put forward explaining the cause of the leak. The assured said that it could have been due to a collision with a submarine. The other party said that it was due to problems that they encountered with the conditions at sea. At first instance it was held that it was not due to lack of maintenance, but due to a collision with a submarine. The loss was therefore occasioned by a peril of the sea and so the insurers were liable.

The Court of Appeal affirmed this, but the House of Lords held that the judge's approach had been unjustified as he should have held that neither explanation was satisfactory as the assured and the insurer had failed to discharge the burden of proof. Thus the claim had to fail.

Another useful case showing the different burdens of proof on the plaintiff is *Captain Ponagous* (1986).

Once it is established that there was the necessary degree of causal link between one of the risks insured against and the loss that happened, one can go on to stage 3.

34. Exemptions

In stage 3, one has to consider whether an otherwise good claim has been spoiled by one of the exemptions in the ICCs clauses 4–7. These relate to piracy (clause 6), strikes (clause 7) and inherent vice (clause 4). The notion of inherent vice is illustrated in *Berk* v. *Style* (1956).

Under clause 5(2) of (A–C), the underwriter waives any breach of the implied warranties of seaworthiness of the ship and fitness of the ship to carry the subject matter insured to the destination, unless the assured or those in his employ are privy to knowledge of such unseaworthiness or unfitness. Thus, the exclusion only operates where the insurer is privy to the unseaworthiness.

Clause 5(2) is an exclusion that only operates where the insurer is privy to knowledge about the ship but clause 5(1) is not, in its entirety, an exclusion clause as it serves to bring everything that relates to the seaworthiness of the vessel into one clause.

Insufficient packing can be regarded as being an inherent vice even if the loss or damage caused was not done by the goods themselves. This will have the effect of depriving the assured of any claims under an insurance policy.

Berk v. *Style* (1956): The insurance policy was for cargo travelling from North Africa to London and there was a specific inherent vice clause in the policy. The cargo contents expanded and burst the bags containing it. Costs were incurred in rebagging the cargo.
It was held that the inherent vice clause related to the bags as well as what they contained so the bags would fall within the inherent vice exclusion.

Section 55(2) of the Marine Insurance Act 1906 states that the insurer is not liable for ordinary wear and tear, ordinary leakage or breakage, inherent vice or nature of the shipmaster insured or for any loss caused by rats or vermin or for any injury to machinery not caused by maritime perils —

Soya v. *White* (1983): The assured, on Cost Insurance Freight terms, bought a large quantity of soya bean meal. The seller said that, for an additional price, he would include a 'heat, sweat and spontaneous combustion' clause. When the cargo arrived at its destination, the beans were heated and in a deteriorated condition, which caused a loss of £700 000.

A claim was made under the old ICCs but the insurers said that the cause of the damage was the result of an inherent vice, which was expressly excluded from being covered by s. 55(2) of the Marine Insurance Act 1906.

It was held that the words 'heat, sweat and spontaneous combustion' all described stages that would lead to fire (each part was an inherent vice of the shipmaster), but the additional peril added to the policy was to cover this particular form of inherent vice. The assured won on the inherent vice point.

In this case, the nature of the risk was also discussed. It was established that, where the moisture content of the soya bean meal was less than 12 per cent on shipment, the need for insurance would not arise, but if it was more than 15 per cent, the deterioration process would always start. In the case, the moisture content was more than 15 per cent and so it was a risk to be insured against. If it was less than 12 per cent there would be no risk and so the claim would not have stood as the loss would not have been caused by an inherent vice.

Types of loss

35. Introduction

It used to be important to know whether a loss was a *total loss* or a *partial loss* because, under the old free from particular average and with particular average policies, some or all forms of partial loss would not be covered.

The use of the term 'particular average loss' meant the same thing as a partial loss. Neither kind of loss was covered unless one of the exceptions to the exclusion could be pleaded.

Under with particular average policies, the particular average loss had to reach a threshold level — *franchise* — or else it would not be covered. Franchise, for example of contractual percentage was 10 per cent and so if 9 per cent loss was suffered, that loss would not be covered unless it fell into one of the exceptions. However, if there was a 12 per cent loss, then the whole 12 per cent would be covered and not just the amount over 10 per cent. Thus only amounts over the trigger point (10 per cent in this example) would be covered, which were called the *excess*.

Since about 1980, the distinction between total and partial loss is irrelevant in the ICCs. However, it can be *actual* or *constructive*.

36. Exception ICC clause 1(1)(3) of (B)

This clause states that the total loss of any package that is lost overboard or dropped while loading on to or unloading from a vessel or craft is not covered.

37. Actual total loss

This is defined in s. 57 of the Marine Insurance Act 1906:

> Where the subject matter insured is destroyed, or so damaged as to cease to be a thing of the kind insured, or where the assured is irretrievably deprived thereof, there is an actual total loss.

The '... or so damaged as to cease ...' arose as a result of the following carriage case —

> *Asfor* v. *Blundell* (1896): A shipment of dates had been carried under a Bill of Lading that made payment due on delivery. The ship sank for a few days and was then refloated and pulled into a London dock.
> The dates looked like dates and had some commercial value for distillation purposes but were no longer merchantable as eating dates. The subject matter had ceased to be a thing of the kind insured and so the carrier was not entitled to payment for the freight.

38. Constructive total loss

According to s. 60(1) of the Marine Insurance Act 1906, constructive total loss occurs when the ship is abandoned because its actual total loss seems unavoidable because it could not be preserved from an actual total loss without expenditure that would have exceeded its value.

In s. 61 of the Act it is stated that where there is a constructive total loss, the assured may either treat the loss as a partial loss or abandon the subject matter insured to the insurer and so treat it as if it were an actual total loss.

In s. 62 of the Act it is stated that, for the assured to claim for a constructive total loss, a notice of abandonment must be given to the insurer. There is no standard form to be used when giving a notice of abandonment but it must be clear and unconditional. However, the insurer does not have to accept it (s. 62(4)).

If he does accept the notice of abandonment, then it is irrevocable (s. 62(6)). This is because the acceptance conclusively admits liability for the loss and that he will pay a total loss claim —

Boon & Chean (1975): The plaintiffs were owners of 668 steel pipes that were insured on free from particular average terms. They were being carried by a barge, which was pulled by a tug. During the voyage the barge was damaged by one of the perils of the sea so that all except 12 of the pipes were lost overside and sank. The remaining 12 were in a damaged condition. The plaintiffs claimed that the cargo was a constructive total loss and it was an actual total loss by application of the 'deminius' principle.

As the policy was on free from particular average grounds, the perils of the sea did not fall within the exceptions to the exclusions to a particular average loss:

The test in clause 13 and s. 60(2)(iii) both have the same effect. The test is whether the cost of recovering, reconditioning and forwarding the goods to the destination would exceed their value on arrival.

Applying this test, the court ruled that the expenses were not greater than the value of the remaining pipes and so the loss was not a constructive total loss. The 'deminius' principle could not be applied to generate an actual total loss. Thus, there could be no claim under the free from particular average policy.

The Bambury (1982): This was a judicial arbitration and Staughton J. was the sole arbitrator.

The ship concerned was a specialised cement carrier.

In September 1980, the ship was carrying cement from Montbassah to an Iraqi port. In December 1980 the ship arrived in the Iraqi port, which was when Iraq was invaded by Iran. The shipmaster was told that the ship could not sail as all vessels had been prohibited from leaving the port. The shipmaster and his crew evacuated the ship.

On 22 December 1980, a skeleton crew returned to live on board the ship. They found that the ship had not been damaged during this time and neither had the authorities asserted any rights. The ship was just stuck.

In October 1981, the shipowner gave a notice of abandonment

to the insurers for a constructive total loss by reason of one of
the perils insured against. The owner's claim was based on s.
60 of the Marine Insurance Act 1906. There was detention of
the ship the cause of which was a peril he had insured against.
It was held that, this was true. There was no necessity to show
physical force as the instruction not to sail was enough.
The question was asked 'Had the owner been deprived of
possession of the ship?' with reference to s. 60 (2)(1) of the Act.
It was held that giving the word 'possession' a liberal
interpretation, the owner had been deprived of possession.
It was also asked whether it was unlikely that the owners could
recover the vessel within a reasonable time.
It was held that it was unlikely as 'reasonable time' is
computed not from the original time of detention, but from
the time of giving the notice of abandonment to the insurers.
Reasonable time in this case was 12 months.

Issues that may arise in marine insurance claims

39. General average

Under the law of carriage, if some act is intentionally done to
prevent a disaster or to mitigate a loss that would otherwise have put
the entire interest at risk, it meant some real cost or sacrifice and
there was objective danger, then that is a general average act.

Under s. 66(2) of the Marine Insurance Act 1906, there is a
general average act where any extraordinary sacrifice or expenditure is voluntarily and reasonably made or incurred in time of peril
for the purpose of preserving the property that is in danger or
difficulty in the common venture. Examples of general average
sacrifices are throwing overboard a cargo to lighten the ship and to
save it and the crew or pulling a ship into a port of refuge for repairs
or contracting for salvage assistance.

If the party claiming the general average action has contributed
in some way to bringing about the situation of danger, then he is
prevented from succeeding with the claim.

Under s. 66(6) of the Act, the insurer is not liable for any general
average loss/contribution where the loss was not incurred for the
purpose of avoiding or in connection with the avoidance of a peril
insured against. However, this section may be contracted out of by
means of the ICCs clause 2:

This insurance covers general average . . . incurred to avoid or in connection with the avoidance of loss from *any cause* except those excluded in . . .

This means that indemnity for a general average contribution is only available where the peril is one insured against under the terms of the policy.

40. Salvage charges

Section 65(2) of the Act states that this means that the charges are recoverable under maritime law by a salvor independently of a contract.

Where salvage activity has been undertaken under a contract, there will be salvage charges in return if it is to prevent a peril insured against.

Section 65 may also be contracted out of by means of the ICCs clause 2 (*ante*).

41. Sue and labour

Under older policies following s. 78 of the Marine Insurance Act 1906, there was a permissive section whereby the assured would be entitled to do various things to preserve the subject matter insured. In the event of doing these things the insurer would compensate the insured.

Sue and labour was considered to be in the nature of a second insurance. Over a period of time, this permissive section became a mandatory obligation on the assured to do certain things in order to minimise any losses incurred. There is now also an obligation on the insurer to reimburse expenses incurred.

The present position is clarified in the ICCs clause 16. Clause 16(1) addresses labour and 16(2) the ability to sue —

The Mammouth Pine (1986): Where cargo had been damaged, there was a short limitation period in the policy within which to bring an action against the carrier, so the assured commenced proceedings in the Japanese courts. He wanted to recover the cost of this from the insurer.
The Privy Council held that this could be done by virtue of clause 16(2), which carried a right to be reimbursed.

Progress test 15

1. Explain each of the following basic principles of insurance:
    - utmost good faith   **(1, 9)**
    - indemnity   **(1, 12)**
    - insurable interest   **(1, 15, 16)**
    - subrogation   **(13)**

2. What happens if the assured fails to disclose all material facts under an insurance policy?   **(2, 8)**

3. What warranties can be contracted out of under the Marine Insurance Act 1906?   **(19)**

4. What are the different types of marine policy?   **(20, 25, 26)**

5. What are the differences and common features of each type of policy?   **(21, 23)**

6. What is the effect of deviating from the agreed voyage? **(28, 29)**

7. How does delay differ to deviation?   **(30)**

8. What are the stages for determining trans-shipment?   **(31–34)**

9. What is a sue and labour clause?   **(41)**

16
Letters of credit

How letters of credit work

1. The main purposes

The main purposes of letters of credit are to provide a means of payment for goods and services supplied by the seller to the buyer and to facilitate dealings between merchants domiciled in different countries by ensuring that payment is made to the seller for the contract of goods or services and that delivery of the goods or services is made to the buyer.

A trader who requires finance for such a transaction may resort to his bank for a *documentary credit*. This is described in article 2 of the Uniform Customs and Practice for Documentary Credits (1974 revision) as:

> ... any arrangement, however named or described, whereby a
> bank (issuing bank) acting at the request and in accordance
> with the customer's instructions is to pay, accept or negotiate.

The documentary credit has also been described by English judges as 'The life and blood of international commerce'. However, payment by such a letter of credit arrangement can only take place if the parties have agreed to it and this has been expressed in the contract. Once a letter of credit arrangement has been provided for in the contract, however, the buyer will then go and ask his bank (issuing bank) to issue a credit in favour of the seller.

The issuing bank can then issue the credit direct to the seller and, by doing so, the seller has the advantage of knowing before he ships the goods that the bank is promising to pay him upon presentation of the correct documents. On the other hand, the disadvantage to the seller is that it may be a foreign bank that issues him with the credit and should that bank then fail to pay under the credit, any proceedings the seller may wish to bring against the bank would have to take place in the same foreign jurisdiction. It is therefore best for the seller for the bank promising payment to be in his own country. Although it is more satisfactory for the seller to have a bank in his own country arranging a credit with the bank in the buyer's country, this is not usually the way things work out. Instead, usually it is the bank in the buyer's country that issues a credit and then routes payment to the seller's bank in the seller's country (the confirming bank).

The bank in the seller's country may be either an advising bank or a confirming bank. A confirming bank is more beneficial to the seller as it means that both the issuing bank and the local confirming bank have promised to honour the payment if the correct documents are provided.

2. The usual process

A seller will present the buyer's documents to his confirming bank and the confirming bank will then pay the seller if the documents are correct.

The confirming bank will then be reimbursed by the issuing bank, which will then be reimbursed by the buyer.

3. Autonomy of a letter of credit

The banks operate under the principle of the 'autonomy' of the letter of credit. This means that they are promising payment if the correct documents are presented. Article 4 of the Uniform Customs and Practice for Documentary Credits (1974 revision) states that the banks deal in documents not in goods or services, which means that banks are not concerned with whether actual performance has been carried out, only that the correct documents have been produced.

The two types of letters of credit

4. Revocable letters of credit

All letters of credit are either *revocable* or *irrevocable*. The contract usually specifies which, but, in the absence of such specification, they will be regarded as revocable letters of credit, as laid down in article 7 of the Uniform Customs and Practice for Documentary Credits (1974 revision).

Revocable letters of credit are used because they are cheaper and can be used to bridge the credit period within the contract. The seller can be sure that there will be no cancellation in close relationships, say, an associated company.

A revocable letter of credit can be sent to a correspondent bank but the beneficiary may have to present documentation as the bank is an agent only of the issuing bank. Under such circumstances, therefore, the correspondent bank is allowed to make payment, which can be very helpful.

However, article 9(a) of the Uniform Customs and Practice for Documentary Credits (1974 revision) must be read subject to article 9(b) which is a proviso to article 9(a). It states that, in effect, the issuing bank is bound to reimburse the confirming bank for any payment made out under the credit.

5. Irrevocable letters of credit

In contrast, article 10 says that an irrevocable letter of credit constitutes a definite undertaking on the part of the issuing bank, subject to the correct documents being presented, and, therefore, such an undertaking cannot be cancelled or amended without the prior agreement of the issuing bank or confirming bank and beneficiary (seller).

If the issuing bank authorises another bank to confirm its irrevocable credit, then it becomes an *irrevocable confirmed letter of credit*, which means that the other bank's confirmation also constitutes a definite undertaking to pay on production of the correct documents — *see Melas* v. *British Imex Industries* (1958): The essential point here was that the parties had to pay despite any conflict regarding the goods as the act of confirming the irrevocable document suggested a definite undertaking to pay against the documents under the principle of the autonomy of the letter of credit.

6. Other types of credit

These include the following, though not demand:

(a) *Sight.* Here the bank is instructed to pay or to arrange for payment to be made against the presentation of correct documents by the seller.

(b) *Time.* Here the bank accepts liability to pay in the future, e.g. 90 days' time. The seller then draws up a Bill of Exchange to mature at that time for, say, goods.

If the seller cannot wait for 90 days, he can negotiate or discount the letter of credit for immediate funds.

(c) *Deferred.* This type was introduced in the Uniform Customs and Practice for Documentary Credits of 1983. Here the beneficiary does not receive immediate payment as the bank promises to pay the seller on the date specified in the letter of credit. There is no need, therefore, for a Bill of Exchange —

> *Forestal Mimosa* v. *Oriental Credit* (1986):In this case, a letter of credit was issued by the Dubai bank and was confirmed by Oriental Credit. The credit required the beneficiaries to draw up 90-day credits. The correct documents were tendered, but the buyer did not honour the drafts.
>
> It was held in the case, with the court referring to article 10 of the Uniform Customs and Practice for Documentary Credits (1974 revision) that Oriental Credit was liable because it had guaranteed its acceptance by confirming the credit and giving a definite undertaking that payment would be made.

(d) *Packing, or, red clause*. Here the credit is available to the seller before he ships the goods. It is paid in two parts:

(*i*) the seller can draw a certain percentage of the funds before the shipment date;

(*ii*) the seller can claim the remainder of the funds once shipment has taken place.

(e) *Revolving credit*. This type of credit is not delineated in the Uniform Customs and Practice for Documentary Credits (1974 revision). Further, the expression is used to describe a number of situations; it is not just one thing. For example, if the seller and buyer have been trading for a while, then the credit will usually be for more than one transaction or £5000 may be credited for one month, but if not all of this quota is used, then the excess may be carried over. If it is used, then the buyer will have to pay again — hence the name revolving credit.

The revolving credit, whether revocable or irrevocable, is the amount that remains constant for a given period. When, during that period, the credit is drawn upon, it will automatically become available again for the full amount.

Payment under a letter of credit

7. Opening a letter of credit

To determine when a letter of credit is to be opened, one usually looks to the sales contract where it is usually specified. However, such specification in the contract may not always be easy to understand and can lead to uncertainty —

State Trading Corporation of India v. *Compagnie Française* (1981):
No mention was made in the contract as to when the letter of
credit was to be established or opened, but, after concluding
the contract, the parties started negotiations to amend it. One
amendment provided that the letter of credit be established
immediately.
It was held that this latter provision was effective and that the
letter of credit was to be established immediately after the
amendment had been agreed.

Under a Cost Insurance Freight contract, the letter of credit is to be
opened at the beginning of the shipment period — *see Pavia* v.
Thurmann-Nielson (1952). This is because the seller is entitled before
he ships the goods to be assured that, on shipment, he will be paid.
The buyer is, therefore, to make the credit available to the seller at
the very first date when the goods may be lawfully shipped.
Sinasson-Teicher v. *Oilcakes and Oilseeds* (1954) extended this rule to
bank guarantees (performance bonds) because they stand on a
similar footing to that of letters of credit. The case also extended the
Pavia ruling saying that the letter of credit or performance bond is
to be opened at a 'reasonable time' before the beginning of the
shipment period. Unfortunately the case did not specify what
'reasonable time' was.

The time issue for opening a letter of credit under an f.o.b.
contract was considered in *Ian Stach* v. *Baker Bosley* (1958) where it
was argued that the time factor may be more critical where there is
a string of sales contracts involved as certainty is needed. However,
the same rule that applies to Cost Insurance Freight contracts was
held to apply to f.o.b. contracts, namely that the letter of credit is to
be established at a reasonable time before the beginning of the
shipment period. This is regardless of what type of f.o.b. contract it
is.

The 'reasonable time' is usually when the confirming bank
notifies the seller that a credit has been opened under the contract in
his favour — *see Bunge Corporation* v. *Vegetable Vitamin Foods Ltd* (1985).

If a letter of credit is *not* opened or not established in time, then
the seller may be able to claim damages from the buyer as the letter
of credit could be a condition of the contract of sale as the ability of
the seller to carry out the transaction will be dependent on the buyer
providing the letter of credit —

Trans-Trust v. *Danubian Trading Co.* (1952): There was a letter of credit payment clause. The buyer failed to open the letter of credit and so there were no goods to perform the contract of sale with. The seller could, therefore, sue for real damages for foreseeable loss of profits. This is calculated under s. 50 of the Sale of Goods Act 1979, depending on the available market.

8. The effect of opening a letter of credit

The effect of opening a letter of credit was set out by Lord Denning in *Alan* v. *El Nasr* (1972). The most likely effect is that it establishes a conditional payment of the price. The consequence of this effect is that the seller must look to the banker first for the payment of the price, so the seller must tender the documents to the bank to obtain payment. If the bank fails to pay, say, because it has become insolvent, then the seller can have recourse to the buyer under the sales contract. The letter of credit is the mechanism, as it is a conditional payment, unless it breaks down and so the documents cannot be presented directly to the bank —

Soprama v. *Marine & Animal By-Products* (1966): Here the seller presented incorrect documents to the banks, which rejected them. By the time the seller had corrected them, it was too late so he wanted to present the documents directly to the buyer instead.
It was held that the buyer could not accept the documents because tender is to be made to the bank in order to receive payment.

If the bank fails to honour the letter of credit because it has become insolvent, then the seller can claim against the buyer under the sales contract — see *Maran Rd.* v. *Austin Taylor* (1975) and *Man* v. *Nigerian Sweets & Confectionery* (1977). The one-off case of *Sale Continuation* v. *Austin Taylor* (1968) ruled that the payment was to be sent directly to the seller when the bank went into liquidation. However, a seller cannot recover direct from the buyer unless the correct documents have been produced — see *Somsher Jute* v. *Sethia* (1987). The seller must fulfil his credit terms in order to be paid.

9. Strict compliance

Under the doctrine of strict compliance, the beneficiary must comply exactly with the terms of the credit in order to obtain payment. Also, the bank must comply with the instructions in the letter of credit in order to be reimbursed. Thus, banks are under no obligation to pay against incorrect documents and, indeed, will not be reimbursed for payments made against incorrect documents. The doctrine is that the documents must be absolutely correct —

> *Equitable Trust Co. of N.Y.* v. *Dawson Partners* (1926): A certificate from just one expert instead of the required two was presented. The bank paid the seller against the document, but could not be reimbursed. Lord Summer in the case said, 'There is no room for documents that are almost the same, or which do just as well'. (The case would be decided differently today because of the introduction of article 18 of the Uniform Customs and Practice for Documentary Credits (1974 revision).)

Because the bank deals in documents rather than goods it cannot be expected to know all the various trade terms and practices of its customers —

> *Rayner* v. *Hambro's Bank* (1943): An invoice stated that coromandel groundnuts were loaded whereas the Bill of Lading phrased it that machine-shelled groundnut kernels had been loaded.
> It was argued by Atkinson J. at the first instance that anyone in the trade would know that the two descriptions meant the same thing.
> The Court of Appeal rejected this and said that a bank cannot be expected to have knowledge of the customs and customary terms. (The case could be decided differently under the Uniform Customs and Practice for Documentary Credits (1974 revision).)

According to the doctrine of strict compliance, it is sufficient that the description of the goods be contained in the set of documents *as a whole* — there is no need for a full description of the goods in *every* document as long as between all the documents there is a full description — *see Midland Bank* v. *Seymour* (1955). As to where the best place for such a description is article 41 of the Uniform Customs and Practice for Documentary Credits (1974 revision) states that the description of the goods must be in the invoice.

10. Payment under reserve

Where the seller tenders non-conforming documents, instead of refusing to accept them, the bank can ask the seller to supply an indemnity, under which the bank will make the letter of credit available — *see Moralice* v. *Mann* (1954).

In contrast, the bank can pay under a *payment under reserve*. This means that the bank reserves the right to reclaim the money without having to justify that there was a good reason for rejecting the documents. The appropriate measure of damages to be awarded for a breach of the bank's undertaking is to be (according to Rowlatt J.) the amount of credit that is the value of material left in the beneficiary's hands.

11. Fraud

In the United Kingdom the issuing bank is not liable if the documents are in order, unless, to its knowledge, the documents or goods are false and the beneficiary or tenderer of the documents was responsible for the falsity.

The courts are slow to intervene in a letter of credit transaction unless it is of sufficiently grave concern. The fraud must be overpowering for the courts to unwind the credit. Also, the fraud must have been established rather than merely alleged. In the case of *Discount Records* v. *Barclays Bank* (1975), fraud was alleged but not established and so the court refused to issue an injunction as it would then be depriving a bona fide third party of payment.

Fraud can be established without having a trial where there has been admittance of the frauds, as in the American case of *Szteijn* v. *Henry Schroeder* (1941), which was referred to and approved in the United Kingdom case of *Edward Owen* v. *Barclays Bank* (1977) concerning Premium Bonds. If there is a clear instance of fraud of which the bank has notice it does not have to pay.

12. Fraud in documents

Within the U.K., if the documents are in order, then the bank must make payment, as we have seen, unless it is known that the documents or goods were false and the beneficiary is responsible for such falsity occurring.

UCM v. *Royal Bank of Canada* (1982): Here the same documents were presented twice with the dates on the Bill of Lading being altered. This gave the bank deemed or actual knowledge of fraud. The bank, therefore, had knowledge of the fraud but could not refuse payment because the fraud was not carried out by the beneficiary, but by a third party.

From this we can see that the fraud has to be carried out by the beneficiary or his agent in order for an injunction to be made against the bank to refuse payment (it does not extend to fraud perpetrated by third parties).

Injunctions will only be granted when the bank knows that any demand for payment that has been or will be made amounts to fraud. Such fraud is to be clear and to the bank's knowledge. Therefore the proof required to get such an injunction is extremely difficult to obtain as the evidence must be clear both as to the *fact* of the fraud and as to the bank's knowledge of it. It is best, therefore, in such instances to have the corroborated evidence of the customer, e.g. by means of the buyer's documents.

This said, the burden of proof required to establish fraud is softening, as was shown in the case of *The United Arab Bank* (1984) where it was held that fraud will not be inferred from mere silence. It must be seen if there are any innocent explanations and, if there are not, then the injunction will be granted. It was also argued in the case that if the beneficiary has the opportunity to respond but does not, then the only reasonable inference will be that of fraud, and then the bank will not have to pay. However, despite this guideline from Ackner L.J., no injunctions have yet been granted in the U.K. to prohibit payment by a bank due to fraud. The *Tukan Timber* v. *Barclays Bank* (1987) case came nearest to succeeding. Fraud was established but there was not the need for an injunction as it was *foreseen* that the documents would be re-tendered.

13. Transport documents

Under article 25 of the Uniform Customs and Practice for Documentary Credits (1974 revision) a combined transport document can be accepted by the bank unless the buyer stipulates otherwise. The transport documents mostly in use today are the Bill of Lading, for combined transport (port to port), and the sea waybill, which provides for delivery to a named consignee or agent upon identification.

The transport document tendered must be a clean one otherwise the bank can reject it, by virtue of article 34, especially the Bill of Lading. To be clean, it must not contain any reservation as to the apparent good order and condition of the goods or the packing — *see British Imex Industries* v. *Midland Bank* (1957).

Banks will accept transport documents that indicate that the goods will be trans-shipped as per article 29 (article 28 covers deck cargo).

Under article 39, if the buyer stipulates to the bank that the insurance document must be for all risks, then, if a certificate is presented bearing ICCs clauses (A), it will amount to all risks.

Thus, the main documents to be called for under a letter of credit are:

(a) the commercial invoice;
(b) transport document;
(c) insurance document.

Depending on the contract of sale, there may be other documents that will be required:

(a) certificate of origin;
(b) certificate of analysis;
(c) packing list;
(d) weight list, etc.

These other documents are dealt with in article 42.

Article 23 stipulates that where documents other than transport, insurance and invoices are required, then the credit should stipulate by whom such documents are to be issued and their wording or data content. If not, the courts will accept the documents as presented —

Commercial Banking Co. of Sydney v. *Jalsard* (1972): Credit was established to cover the cost of Christmas tree lights. The credit required the beneficiary to produce a certificate of inspection, along with other documents. This was done and the bank paid against them. The bank then sought reimbursement but the beneficiary refused, contending that there should have been an electrical inspection to make sure that the lights were working.

It was held that the beneficiary should have specified that he wanted an electrical inspection in the letter of credit. The beneficiary, therefore, had to pay.

The bank must therefore check that each document complies with the terms of the letter of credit and that they are internally consistent. The standard required is that of reasonable care (article 15) —

Gian Singh v. *Bank de L'Indochine* (1974): Here a certificate and passport were presented for the bank's inspection. The bank accepted the documents but they were, in fact, forgeries. The bank later tried to gain its reimbursement from the buyer but he refused to pay.

It was held that the bank was to be reimbursed by the buyer because the bank had exercised reasonable care in examining the documents, which appeared to be correct on their face. This sufficed, despite the forgery. Lord Diplock stated,

'. . . visual inspection of the documents presented is all that is called for'.

If documents tendered to the bank are incorrect, then, under article 46, they can be corrected and re-tendered as long as this occurs before the end of the expiry date. In the case of *The Lena* (1981), it was held that the bank is not estoppel from finding further discrepancies — here two were found. The documents also must be presented soon enough after shipment has taken place or else the bank can reject them.

Progress test 16

1. Name some types of letters of credit.   **(4, 6)**

2. What are the main objectives of a letter of credit?   **(1)**

3. Why have they been described as the 'life and blood of international commerce?   **(1, 2)**

4. What is the principle of 'autonomy of credit'?   **(3)**

5. What is an irrevocable letter of credit? Why are these used? **(4, 5)**

6. What are the rules for opening and closing a letter of credit? **(6, 7)**

7. What is the effect of the doctrine of strict compliance?   **(8)**

8. What effect does fraud have on a letter of credit?   **(10, 11)**

9. 'In documentary credit operations all parties concerned deal in documents and not in goods' (article 4, the Uniform Customs and Practice for Documentary Credits 1983). Discuss.

17

Remedies for breaches of contract

Introduction

1. Are there remedies for both buyer and seller?
Should there be a breach of an international trade contract then
there *are* remedies for both buyer and seller.

The buyer's remedies

2. What these are
A buyer can reject either the documents or the goods if there has
been a breach of contract.

3. Rejection
The two rights of rejection are separate although if one of the
documents reveals a defect but a buyer still accepts them, he cannot
reject for that defect at a later date —

Panchaud Frères v. *Establissement Général Grain Co.* (1970):
There was a Cost Insurance Freight contract for grain to be
shipped from a Brazilian port in June or July 1965. In
addition to Cost Insurance Freight documents, the seller had
to tender a certificate of quality to the buyer. When the
documents were handed over, the Bill of Lading said that the
goods had been shipped on 31 July, but the certificate of
quality said that they had been loaded on 10–12 of July.
The buyer accepted the documents but later rejected the
goods due to the late shipment.
The issue was whether the buyer was aware of the late
shipment.
The Court of Appeal held that the buyer was estoppel from
rejecting the goods; the buyer should have been suspicious, he
should have looked at the documents as a whole, he would

then have realised that the shipment took place outside the contracted period.

Cross L.J. in the case emphasised the point that any reasonable person who read the documents would have seen that the goods were not shipped in the contractual period. The buyer should have inspected the documents carefully before accepting the goods.

The Kwek Tek Chao v. *British Traders & Shippers* (1954): There was a contract for the sale of chemicals Cost Insurance Freight Hong Kong that stipulated that shipment was to be no later than 31 October from a Continental port.

The goods were shipped in early November, but the Bill of Lading was falsely dated, showing shipment taking place on 31 October. The documents were presented through a bank to the buyer's bank, everything seemed in order and payment was made against the documents.

Before the goods arrived in Hong Kong, the buyer learnt that the vessel had not been loaded until early November.

When the goods arrived, the buyer accepted them and put them in a warehouse but later said that they had discovered the false dating of the Bill of Lading. They then sought to reject the documents. The market had meanwhile fallen in this commodity and they could not make a profit.

It was held that the buyer could not reject the goods as he had already accepted them. However, he still had a remedy against the seller as he could still claim damages for the incorrect documents. The false dating of the Bill of Lading deprived the buyer of his right to reject; if it had had the correct date he could have rejected the document. The seller argued that it was too late for the buyer to complain about the documents because he had accepted the goods.

Lord Devlin held that these two rights of rejection were independent. Although the buyer accepted the goods, this could not prejudice his rights *vis-à-vis* the documents. The property passed to the buyer was only so passed on condition that it fell in line with the contract. The buyer was, therefore, entitled to damages for the loss of his right to reject the documents from the seller. The measure of damage was the difference between the contracted price of the goods and their market value when they realised the false dating of the Bill of Lading in Hong Kong.

4. Action for non-delivery

Section 51 of the Sale of Goods Act 1979 regulates the measure of damages to be applied for non-delivery. Applied to a Cost Insurance Freight contract, what is crucial is not the time of the delivery of the *goods*, but the time of the delivery of the documents that *represent* the goods.

If the seller does not ship the goods, the measure is the market value of the documents —

> *Sharpe* v. *Nosawa* (1917): There was a contract for the sale of Japanese peas Cost Insurance Freight London, which were to be shipped in June. Evidence showed that if they were shipped on the last day of June, the documents would take three weeks to reach London but the goods would take two months. The seller failed to ship the goods and the buyer sued for damages. It was held that the difference between the contract price and the market price in London in the second half of July was the measure of damages that the seller had to give the buyer.

> *Garnac Grains* v. *Faure Fairclough* (1961): There was a sale of goods contract from the US, Cost Insurance Freight UK. They were to be shipped at the end of December or beginning of January. If they were shipped on the last day of January, they would be in the UK by 4 February; if not, the buyer was able to buy the goods elsewhere.
> It was held that the measure of damages was the difference between the contract price and market price in London on 4 February.

The measure of damages as given in s. 51 (3) of the Sale of Goods Act is prima facie and so can be waived depending on the circumstances of the case or if the terms of the contract state how the damages are to be assessed —

> *Toepfer* v. *Cremer* (1975): The contract specified that, in the event of default, the buyer would be entitled to damages, and that these would be based upon the actual or estimated value of the goods on the date of default.
> The issue in the case was what exactly was meant by 'date of default' — was it the last day on which the seller could perform his obligations or the next day thereafter? This mattered a great deal as the market price changed rapidly.
> It was held by the Court of Appeal that 10 July was the day, i.e.

the last day on which the seller could perform his obligations and give a notice of appropriation.

Bremer v. *Vanden* (1978): The House of Lords debated exactly the same clause as above, but took the opposite approach and assessed damages as beginning on 11 July.
Lord Wilberforce considered that the buyer could only buy from elsewhere on 11 July. (This House of Lords case overrules *Toepfer* v. *Cremer* (1975) (*ante*).)

5. Anticipatory breaches

The Tai Hing Cotton Mill v. *Kamsing Knitting Factory* (1978) case raises the question of how s. 51 (3) is to be applied in situations where there is an anticipated breach of contract by the seller. That the seller is going to breach the contract can usually be ascertained from indications from the seller that he has no intention of performing the contract. For example, he may say, 'I will not deliver the goods on ...' The buyer can then either accept the anticipated breach or hold the seller to the contract.

It was held in this case that the measure of damages was the difference between the contract and market price in December, when the seller should have delivered.

Another example is *The Playa Larga* case —

The Playa Larga (1983): The contract was for the sale of sugar between Cuban and Chilian companies that was entered into in early 1973. In September 1973, there was a coup in Chile and the regime was overthrown. The vessel, 'The Playa Larga', had stopped in a Chilian port to unload the cargo when the coup took place.
The Cuban seller ordered the ship to leave port without unloading the cargo, so the vessel sailed away. The main issue in the case was what remedy the buyer had got for not receiving all the goods.
It was held that the buyer was entitled to damages for the seller's breach of contract. There is an implied term under s. 12 of the Sale of Goods Act 1979 that the buyer shall have quiet possession of the goods and that the seller will not interfere with the buyer's possession of the goods. The seller by his actions had done so and therefore had breached s. 12. There was also a tort of conversion, although he did not have to use it as he had a contractual obligation, but although he did not use tort, arguably he could have succeeded if he had.

6. Further remedies available to the buyer

If s. 1 of the Bills of Lading Act 1855 does not operate, then there can still be an *implied contract* between the buyer and carrier and so the buyer may have a contractual claim against the carrier.

7. The position under tort

The position under tort is illustrated well in *The Wear Breeze* (1967) case. The carrier failed to properly fumigate the ship, so the cargo was damaged as a result. The holder of the delivery order tried to sue the carrier, but there was no implied contract so he tried to sue under tort but this also failed.

The court determined that the carrier only owed a duty of care to someone who had property in the goods or the right to possession at the time of the tort. This is well-established that a person only owes a duty of care with regard to property to its owners or to those who have the right to the property.

However, in the case of *Irene's Success* (1981) the judge refused to follow the decision given in the case of *The Wear Breeze*. He took the view that the law of negligence had changed, particularly in the light of *Anns* v. *Merton London Borough Council* (1977). The House of Lords said that there is a range of situations where a duty of care can arise. Lord Wilberforce said that it can arise where it is foreseeable that negligence will occur, or if there is a policy reason. (This may now be affected by *Murphy* v. *Brentwood* 1991.) In *The Nea Tyhi* (1982) case, the judge did say that, if he had to, he would follow the case of *Irene's Success*.

Thus there was a state of confusion in the law from 1981. The decision as to whom the duty of care was owed depended on the judge in each case, but, in 1986, the case of *The Aliakmon* clarified the position. At the first instance, the judge recognised a duty of care, but the House of Lords and Courts of Appeal reaffirmed the decision that had been given in *The Wear Breeze* case, that the carrier does not owe a duty of care to the Cost Insurance Freight buyer.

The case established that a carrier only owes a duty of care to the owner of the goods or the person who has possession of the property at the time of the tort. It should be noted that a carrier can be sued for other actions beside the tort of negligence, e.g. he can be sued for the tort of conversion, or for misrepresentation —

The Saudi Crown (1986): In this case, a Bill of Lading was falsely dated; the goods should have been loaded between 15 June and July, but the cargo was, in fact, loaded later than 15 July.

The buyer was presented with the documents and they accepted and paid for them. Before the goods arrived, the buyer realised that the goods had been shipped late. The buyer claimed damages against the carrier for false dating of the Bill of Lading. It was held that the carrier was liable. The buyer was deceived into accepting illegal documents and suffered losses that he would not have done had the dates been true.

The seller's remedies

8.   What these are

A seller has remedies against the goods or the buyer. The key statutory provisions are given in ss. 44–46 of the Sale of Goods Act 1979, which state that the seller has the right, if the buyer becomes insolvent, to stop the goods in transit, which means he can have the right to the goods until the price is paid. The main action brought against buyers is for the price of the goods.

Under s. 49 of the Act, if property passes to the buyer, then the seller can sue. Section 49 (2) qualifies s. 49 in that, if there is a fixed date in the contract for payment, payment must be made whether the property has passed or not; if not the seller can sue the buyer.

9.   Non-acceptance

Damages for wrongful non-acceptance are covered in s. 50 of the Sale of Goods Act 1979. There are two possible claims for damages for the buyer's non-acceptance of documents. Section 50 (3) states that damages shall be the difference between the market and contracted price at the time when the documents have been delivered. (The time of presentation of the documents is, therefore, relevant here.) The courts will look at the market at the Cost Insurance Freight destination if the buyer refuses to take up the documents —

> *Muller McLean* v. *Leslie and Anderson* (1921): Goods were to be shipped from New York to Calcutta. The buyer was a London merchant and the documents had to be presented to him in London. He refused to take them up.
>
> It was held that the seller was to be awarded damages for the difference between the contracted and market price at Calcutta.

Progress test 17

1. What are the buyer's main remedies for breach of an international trade contract?   **(1–4, 6)**

2. What is the effect of s. 51 of the Sale of Goods Act 1979?   **(4)**

3. What is the position under the Law of Tort?   **(7)**

4. Does a seller have any remedies available? If so, what are they? **(8, 9)**

18
English arbitration

The mechanism for arbitration appeals

1. Pre 1979
Pre 1979, there existed a case stated procedure, governed by the Arbitration Act 1950, but it proved to amount to no more than a delaying tactic used to avoid the paying of awards.

General dissatisfaction was made known by various judges and proposals were submitted for a new procedure to be introduced. In a report in 1978 under the chairmanship of Lord Donaldson (Command No. 7284), the main recommendation was that reasons should be given for awards.

2. The Arbitration Act 1979
As a result the Arbitration Act 1979 came into effect, abolishing the old case stated procedure by virtue of s. 1. It also allows appeals to be made to the courts on questions of law arising from awards made as a result of arbitration agreements (s. 1(2)). The courts can then confirm, vary, set aside the award or remit it for reconsideration by the arbitrator. Section 1(3) states that the appeal must be with the consent of all parties.

Reasons must be given in sufficient detail to enable the court to consider any question of law, should there be any appeal (s. 1(5)).

3. Leave of appeal
There needs to be a grant of leave if a party wishes to appeal. Lord Diplock in *The Antaios* v. *Salen Rederierna* (1985) case stated that leave is only to be granted where there is a need for amplification, elucidation or adaptation to changing practices relating to existing guidelines laid down by Appellant Courts. The aim is to create a more definite framework and to deal quickly, briefly, yet effectively with matters.

Leave should not be granted for appeal by the High Court,

unless, after considering all the circumstances, they find that the question of law could substantially affect the rights of the party(s) to the agreement (s. 1(4)). However, judges have tried to lay down even more stringent conditions, as illustrated by *The Nema* (1981) case where Lord Denning in the Court of Appeal laid down *obiter* guidelines as to when leave was to be granted. He distinguished between one-off contracts and standard-form contracts that are likely to recur. He stated that leave should be granted in one-off situations, as in *The Nema*, unless it was apparent to the judge that the meaning ascribed to the clause was wrong. In standard-form contracts, leave is only to be granted if there is strong prima-facie evidence to show that the arbitrator was wrong.

However, Goff J. refused to follow *The Nema* guidelines in later cases (*The Evia* (1981) and *The Rio Sun* (1981)). *The Nema* case, though, was the first to go to the House of Lords under the new procedure. There Lord Diplock adopted Denning's approach. The case of *The Antaios* v. *Salen Rederierna* (1985) later confirmed *The Nema* guidelines.

4. Refusal to grant leave

In *Aden Refinery* v. *Ugland Management Co.* (1987) the issue raised was whether refusal by a judge to grant leave to appeal allows the dissatisfied party to go directly to the Court of Appeal. The Court of Appeal held that, under s. 1(6)(a) of the Arbitration Act 1979, leave of appeal is necessary.

Arbitration in international commercial disputes

5. International commercial disputes

Arbitration need not follow the same procedure as that conducted in a court of law as long as it does not lead to any unfairness in the area. Most commercial disputes are resolved by arbitration rather than litigation.

6. The qualities of an international arbitrator

Those appointed as international arbitrators must have certain qualities:

(a) They must have the legal knowledge and capacity to conduct the arbitration.

(b) The parties to the international contract must not have imposed any restrictions on the arbitrator. It is therefore usually best for arbitrators to be appointed *after* the dispute has arisen. For example, within the Grain and Feed Trade Association, their rule 3 imposes restrictions, as does the Federation of Oils, Seeds and Fats Association, which stipulates that the '... person must be a commercial man'. Such phrasing is vague and has been interpreted differently by lawyers in the U.K. Essentially they mean that practising members of the legal profession cannot be appointed, as in the case of *Pandora Co.* (1975).

(c) The arbitrator must not be restricted by the applicable law. For example, in Columbia, the arbitrator must be a Columbian national whereas in Saudi Arabia the arbitrator appointed must be of Muslim religion.

(d) Each party of a dispute will decide on the qualifications they require the arbitrator to possess. The usual practice is to appoint lawyers in international commercial disputes.

(e) The arbitrator must have adequate knowledge of the language of the country where the arbitration is to take place in order to be able to understand and examine witnesses.

(f) The experience and outlook of the arbitrator is important. The person appointed must be trained in public international law rather than just his own country's domestic law.

7. The powers of an arbitrator

The exercising of an arbitrator's powers can rarely be tested by the courts, making an arbitrator very powerful in a dispute. His powers will derive from the local law and will of the parties. Although the parties can define the limits of the arbitrator, they cannot really define the limits of his powers.

Some of the more important powers are:

(a) to order pleadings at any time;
(b) to fix dates for hearings;
(c) to grant postponements at any time or stage in the proceedings;
(d) to proceed with hearings in the absence of a party;
(e) to order discovery and inspection of documents, property and premises;
(f) to consult with other persons.

8. The arbitration agreement

The arbitrator is bound by the wording of the expressed agreement. If the agreement is not expressed, then the inference will be drawn from the conduct of the parties.

The agreement will usually have a provision stating that disputes, if any, should be referred to one of the following institutions:

(a) London Court of Arbitration (LCA);
(b) International Chamber of Commerce (ICC);
(c) International Centre for Settlement of Investment Disputes (ICSID);
(d) Multinational Investment Guarantee Agency (MIGA).

However, there is no specification as to the law to be chosen to decide the dispute, although there may be a separate clause covering the issue. For example such a clause could read, 'to be according to United Kingdom law'.

9. The terms of reference

These should include details such as the full names and addresses of the parties and the arbitrator, a summary of the parties' respective claims, a definition of the issues to be determined by the arbitrator, and an indication of the place of arbitration. If the parties should choose a federal country (United States), for example, then they should specify the state (New York).

The terms of reference are to be signed by the parties to the dispute and the arbitrator. Once signed, the document constitutes an agreement to arbitrate, although in theory the parties may refuse to sign.

10. National law

This national law sets the limits within which the arbitrator can act. There are two limits:

(a) by deciding which matters are not included in the arbitration procedure;
(b) by establishing a system of procedures.

The parties involved in arbitration must stipulate the place of arbitration. An example could be London, but some countries do agree 'freedom of choice', such as France. If a place is *not* stipulated, the arbitrator should apply the law designated as the proper law by national law.

11. Miscellaneous sources of an arbitrator's power

Other sources of an arbitrator's power are the habitual conduct of proceedings in various trades, the appointment of an arbitrator by a third party (e.g., the Organisation for Economic Co-operation and

Development or the United Nations Commission on International Trade Law) and public policy.

12. Rules of evidence

The rules of evidence differ in Civil and Common Law countries and so the jurisdiction where a dispute is to be settled must be chosen with care. In Civil Law countries, counsel must submit a list of articles as proof, along with a list of witnesses, they must seek the judge's leave in order to call the witnesses and only a judge can examine a witness and counsel can only present questions via the judge.

Differences also exist as to the examination of the parties. In civil law countries, the party is not treated as a witness and so the judge is not required to pay attention to what a party may have said to support the case. Counsel can obtain discovery only of specific documents and needs to obtain leave for discovery. It must be established that the particular document(s) exists and that it is in the possession of the party referred to. In a Common Law country on the other hand, like the United Kingdom, all documents may be taken to obtain the one actually needed.

Progress test 18

1. What was the mechanism for English arbitration appeals prior to 1979? **(1)**

2. What effect has the Arbitration Act 1979 had on the area? **(2)**

3. What are the main provisions of the statute? **(2–4)**

4. What qualities are required to become an arbitrator? **(6)**

5. What powers does an arbitrator have? **(7)**

6. Where does the power of the arbitrator come from? **(8, 11)**

19
Conflict of international laws

Laws, conventions, treaties

1. The Civil Jurisdiction and Judgments Act 1982

The origin of the Act — which came into full force on 1 January 1987 — lies in the Treaty of Rome (1957). Article 220 of the Treaty strives to facilitate the free movement of judgments within the EC. It is viewed as being a welcome step towards EC integration and the development of private international law.

2. An overview of the main sections of the 1982 Act

These are as follows:

(a) *Section 1*. This section defines the Brussels Convention and the term contracting states.

(b) *Section 2*. The section states how the Conventions are to be interpreted in accordance with decisions of the European Court of Justice. The U.K. courts can also consider the *Jenard and Schlosser Reports* (1979) for guidance.

(c) *Sections 4–8*. These contain supplementary provisions as to the enforcement in the U.K. of judgments given in other contracting states regarding the Conventions. Section 4 allows a judgment creditor to obtain a mareva injunction as a protective measure against the debtor's property, pending determination of a dispute as to its jurisdiction, etc. This is covered further in ss. 24–28.

(d) *Sections 10, 16, 17*. These sections confer jurisdiction on the courts generally in a specified contracting state of the Brussels Convention. They also include provisions for allocating jurisdiction among the courts within the U.K.

Exceptions do exist within s. 16. For example, the U.K. courts will have exclusive jurisdiction where the dispute is principally concerned with title to land situated in the U.K.

(e) *Sections 18, 19*. Section 18 has provisions for the enforcement in each part of the U.K. of judgments given in other parts, these extend to non-money payments according to schedule 7 of the Act. However, s. 19 excludes and modifies s. 18 by excluding jurisdiction review by certain courts.

(f)   *Section 30*. This section confers on the English courts jurisdiction to entertain proceedings for torts against a foreign land, unless the proceedings mainly concern a question of title or the right to possess land.

(g)   *Sections 31–38*. These contain a number of provisions relating to judgments enforced in a non-contracting state.

(h)   *Sections 41–46*. These sections concentrate on definitions of domicile with regard to an individual, corporation, association or trust.

(i)   *Section 49*. This provides that a U.K. court has discretion as to whether to stay or dismiss proceedings before it, on the grounds of forum non conveniens, i.e. it considers another court as being more convenient or appropriate to settle the dispute.

3.   Amendments made to the Civil Jurisdiction and Judgments Act 1982 in 1991

These were as follows:

(a)   The new s. 3 — extension. Section 3 of the 1982 Act is to be extended by a new s. 3(A)(1)(2) and s. 3(B)(1)(2). The effect of s. 3(A) generally is to implement the Lugano Convention 1988 (*see* 19:8) into U.K. law between EC and EFTA states. Section 3(B) addresses the meanings to be attached to the new Convention. The U.K. courts are to follow the decisions of the Lugano Contracting State Courts and reports are made (by Jenard & Moller OJ 1990 c 189/57) in order to ascertain the meanings and overall effects of decisions taken there.

(b)   Amendments to s. 9 and article 54(B). Section 9 of the 1982 Act is to be amended. In addition a new s. 1(A) is to be inserted that it will be used where there is doubt as to whether it is the Brussels or Lugano Convention that should apply. The courts are to resort to provisions in article 54(B) of the Lugano Convention if this situation occurs. Article 54(B) outlines that the Lugano Convention applies where the defendant is domiciled in a non-EC state or when proceedings are started in one of these such states.

(c)   Section 2 of the 1991 Act. This section of the Act is responsible for amending s. 1 of the 1982 Act. It substitutes the words 'the conventions' with the 'Brussels Conventions'. It also introduces definitions as to what is a Brussels or Lugano contracting state, along with one for the Lugano Convention itself.

4. Brussels Convention 1968

The Civil Jurisdiction and Judgments Act 1982 also implemented the Brussels Convention on jurisdiction and the enforcement of judgments in civil and commercial matters. The Brussels Convention was signed by the six original EC member states in 1968 and it came into force in 1973.

5. Brussels Convention 1978

It was necessary to amend the Convention when the U.K. entered the EC. It was amended in 1978 and implemented together with the Civil Jurisdiction and Judgments Act on 13 July 1982, abolishing the 1968 provisions. The new 1978 Convention, referred to as the Accession Convention, along with the Greek Accession Convention of the same year, laid down a set of rules that the EC courts have to apply in order to settle a dispute where the defendant is domiciled in a contracting state, that is, a member of the EC that has adopted the Convention.

6. Domicile

The concept of 'domicile' as used in the Convention differs from the English concept. The 1982 Act has therefore adopted a special definition for this purpose under ss. 41–46. Under s. 41, the domicile of individuals is taken to be akin to residence and under s. 42, the domicile of a corporation is based on the seat of the company, 'seat' being further defined in s. 42(3)(a) and (b).

7. The Lugano Convention and the EFTA states

The Lugano Convention applies when the defendant is domiciled, or the judgment is to be enforced between an EC and EFTA (European Free Trade Association) state. Examples of EFTA states are Austria, Iceland, Finland, Switzerland, Sweden and Norway.

8. The effect of the Lugano Convention

The Lugano Convention is also called the Parallel Convention because it was modelled on the Brussels EC Conventions. It amends the 1982 Act in different ways. For example, under the 1982 Act a writ is needed along with Common Law and statutory rules to decide a judgment — these disappear in the new regime.

There is to be a new 1991 revised Civil Jurisdiction and Judgments Act, due to be in effect by the end of 1992/early 1993. The 1991 version, as did the 1982, adheres to the terms in the Treaty of Rome facilitating the free movement of judgments across Western and Central Europe.

9. Protocol

A protocol on the interpretation of the Brussels Convention of 1968 was signed by the same six member states at Luxembourg in 1971 and this came into force in the same states in 1975.

10. Treaties

Those outside the EC can still have judgments enforced against them in other states in the EC. This has put such states in a weaker position. However, article 59 of the Brussels Convention of 1978 allows for special treaties to be made between member and non-member states, but very few have come into effect.

11. Spain and Portugal become members of the EC Convention

On 26 May 1989, another Accession Convention, called the Donosta San Sebastian Convention, was signed with Spain and Portugal to bring all members of the EC in line with the Brussels Convention. This is yet to be ratified, but when it is it will come into effect through the Civil Jurisdiction and Judgments Act by means of an Amendment Order. Once in force it will implement the Convention into the U.K.'s version of the Act.

12. Interpretation of the Lugano Convention

EFTA states are not bound by the judgments of the European Court of Justice as they are not members of the EC. Thus the Court has no jurisdiction over signatories of the Lugano Convention and neither are they parties to the 1971 Protocol.

However, should an EFTA state decide to become a member of the EC, it will then have to accept the Brussels Conventions and the Protocol, thus granting the Act jurisdiction over disputes. There is the possibility that the EFTA states will become part of the EC and that Eastern European and Commonwealth countries will become part of the Lugano Convention.

The U.K. has ratified the 1988 Lugano Convention. The only EFTA state to have ratified the Convention so far is Switzerland. The Convention came into force between Switzerland and the U.K. on 1 May 1992. The main object of the Convention is to make it easier to enforce one state's judgments in the courts of the other states.

Therefore, as a result of a conference held in Lugano, EFTA states are now able to enjoy the same advantages in terms of the enforcement of judgments that contracting states of the Brussels Convention enjoy. The Lugano Convention was needed as EFTA states were reluctant to the European Court of Justice intervening to control decisions. The Lugano Convention will therefore operate alongside the Brussels Convention.

Progress test 19

1. Why is the Treaty of Rome so important to the Civil Jurisdiction & Judgments Act of 1982? **(1, 8)**

2. What effect did the Brussels Convention of 1968 and 1978 have on the area of conflict? **(4, 5)**

3. What is the meaning of domicile under the 1982 Act? **(6)**

4. Give examples of EFTA states. **(7)**

5. What will be the future effect of the Lugano Convention? **(8)**

6. What is the effect of the Donosta San Sebastian Convention 1989? **(11)**

Appendix
Examination technique

1. Preparation and revision

To a certain extent the preparation and revision required for International Trade Law is the same as for other law subjects. Study past examination papers carefully. They should reveal the subject areas which are considered important (although there may be some variation from year to year, with emphasis on current issues). Attempt questions from past papers, taking care to gain practice in timing individual answers.

2. Source

Prior to analysing a statute, it is always worthwhile to read Law Commission papers, working papers, and reports which were published prior to the Bill receiving royal assent. Academic commentaries in journals and law periodicals are also very useful.

3. Statutory materials

Acts of Parliament are paramount in International Trade Law. It is therefore essential to become acquainted with words and main sections of the statutes which form part of the area of research or revision to be undertaken. It would be advisable for students to purchase a personal copy of any relevant legislation; for courses which are post graduate, a copy of Incoterms would also be required. Become confident in handling the statutes, to avoid wasting time trying to find the place. Do not copy out passages from statutes unless the question requires a detailed consideration of the wording, but summarise the legal principles, by reference to the relevant articles.

4. Cases

When referring to a case state briefly the legal principle decided and the name of the case. It is rarely necessary to state the facts at length, although a brief exposition of the facts may be helpful.

5. The examination

Do not rush into answering any questions but allow yourself time to read through the whole paper carefully before writing. You may be allowed 'reading time' before the start of the examination. Make good use of this time to read and think.

It is often helpful, after choosing the questions to be answered, to write a rough outline first, noting relevant provisions from the relevant legislation and decided cases. After completing the answer, cross out the rough work.

Decide in advance how much time you should spend on each question and keep to it. It is easy to spend too long on the first question, particularly if it is an essay, and to run out of time on the last. If time is very short, it is better to write an outline of an answer in note form than to leave the question uncompleted.

If you finish the examination early do not leave the examination room but use the time to read over your answers and make corrections.

6. Essays and problem questions

As with most law examinations, questions may usually be divided into essay and problem questions.

An essay question is often formulated as a quotation followed by the word 'Discuss'. A similar approach should be adopted to both types of questions:

(a) identify the relevant subject area;
(b) state the relevant law;
(c) apply the law to the facts (problem) or discuss the law (essay);
(d) state your conclusion.

Always keep the wording of the question in front of you and make sure you answer it. It is easy to lose track of the question.

Problem questions involve the application of the law to hypothetical facts. Do not make any assumptions about facts omitted, but consider alternatives. It may be necessary to go through the process from (a) to (d) several times during the question before reaching a final conclusion. *Never* state the conclusion first and work backwards, a sure sign of inexperience. The examiner is more interested in the process (identification, analysis and application of the law) than in reaching the 'right' conclusion. (The question may have been set in a 'grey' area in which there is no single answer.)

Index